Million Hal

CW00458328

27 Powerful Habits to Wire Your Mind for Success, Become Truly Happy, and Achieve Financial Freedom.

Stellan Moreira

About the Author

Stellan Moreira is young and motivated entrepreneur and best-selling author on a mission to change himself, and the world.

While he may be young, his information is valuable. He is self-educated, and he plans on instilling a certain sense of understanding within each reader that he has been fortunate to be able to instill within himself. This understanding has allowed him to accomplish so much, and keeps him constantly looking forward with gratitude, understanding, and determination to reach all his goals. Not only this, but it has allowed him to truly understand himself, and find a beautiful sense of peace and happiness he has always longed for. From this point onward, he realized that we wanted and needed to share his values, thoughts, information, and beliefs with the rest of the world. He realized that each individual has a meaningful purpose, and he put it upon himself to place great effort towards helping as many people find and realize their own.

His sincere mission and purpose is to help as much as he possibly can. He wants you to do the best in everything, and he wants you to succeed. What most people don't realize is that they already possess all the powers needed to make their lives completely filled with happiness, peace, wealth, and abundance, and the only thing truly standing in their way is themselves: the limiting thoughts and beliefs that they harbor in their minds. These beliefs tell them that they can't accomplish their dreams, that they can't be happy, and that they can't live the life they wish they were meant for. He is here to tell you right now that these thoughts are beyond untrue. They are so false, and yet we constantly allow them to successfully blind each and every one of us from our true potential.

Stellan is here to completely change this. He is here to make a difference in each and every readers lives.

He will never stop, for this is only the beginning.

The power of the mind is limitless; utilize it, and live a life beyond worth living.

-   Stellan Moreira

This book is dedicated to those who support and believe in us, and also to those who don't. You fuel our mental drive and motivate us every day, and for that we shall be forever **grateful**.

Thank you.

Follow <u>StellanMoreira</u> for book updates & free offers, inspiring content, motivational stories, and other resources to help you wire your "growth" mentality, achieve profound success, and *"live a life beyond worth living."*

 <u>StellanMoreira</u>

 <u>StellanMoreira</u>

 <u>StellanMoreira</u>

Million Dollar Habits

By

Stellan Moreira

information is without contract or any type of guarantee assurance.

The trademarks that are used are without any consent, and the publication of the trademark is without permission or backing by the trademark owner. All trademarks and brands within this book are for clarifying purposes only and are the owned by the owners themselves, not affiliated with this document.

Table of Contents

15

Introduction

Thank you for taking time to read this. This book is filled with information that will **completely** change your life, but only if you implement what it teaches.

P.S. Pay attention to the **bold**.

"We are what we repeatedly do. Excellence, therefore, is not an act but a habit." – *Aristotle*

This quote is indeed very true: Our habits define us and shape our lives. If we excel at what we do, live a harmonious life, and are at peace, we can thank the healthy and positive habits we have built over the course of our life. If, however, we are unproductive, addicted to unhealthy practices, and surrounded by chaos, then for that too, we can thank our habits.

If you are looking for **life altering** information, look no further. This book will provide you with the proper information and guidance that will not only allow you, but push you towards completely changing your life for the better. This book will not only give you the information, but aid you towards understanding every bit of it. This book will be your **mentor** to success. Allow it to be so, and you will experience a life **beyond** worth living.

You may not know me, but there's two things that I can absolutely say I know about you:

1.   You can achieve **ANYTHING**.

2.   **YOU** can **CHANGE** the **WORLD**.

You may not know it yet, but I do.

By reading this book, you are not only helping yourself, but me as well. For my sincere mission and purpose is to instill within each reader a sense of understanding that I have been fortunate to be able to instill within myself. This sense of understanding has allowed me to accomplish so much, and keeps me constantly striving to achieve **all** my goals. Not only this, but it has also allowed me to truly understand myself, and find a beautiful sense of peace and happiness that I have always longed for.

First step in achieving this: **self-improvement**.

Continue reading this book, and you will accomplish exactly that.

The Life-Changing Power of Habit

It is estimated that about 95% of the things we do daily are derived from nothing other than **pure habit.** Waking up in the morning and immediately grabbing your phone, waiting to do your homework until late at night, having breakfast with the same drink every day, and going to work and taking a specific route to get there are all examples of habitual activities: each of which have their own personalized touch to them. As humans, we are absolute **creatures of habit**.

The habits we possess can influence us in neutral, positive, and negative manners. While the neutral ones do not have any substantial effect on our lifestyle, the positive and negative ones shape the **entire** course of our life.

While a negative habit can slow your progress and adversely influence your lifestyle, a positive habit can greatly improve it. It can bring positivity, possibilities, progress, health, wealth, abundance, happiness, love, and success into your life. It can change the type of person you are from head to toe, and, in consequence, change your **entire** reality. That is the **power of habit.**

How exactly does that happen? How do we form habits? Do we have any power over habit development? Is habit formation a conscious process? These and many other such questions may be running through your mind.

Habit formation is usually a conscious process; however, if we repeat a behavior long enough, usually for a month or so, it becomes a part of our routine, at which point it becomes a habit of our subconscious.

Additionally, when we are around certain people or are exposed to environmental factors, we automatically (without conscious effort) pick on the behaviors of others and imbed them into our subconscious, thereby reforming and shaping our current habits. For instance, if one of your colleagues pronounces a word you have never heard before a certain way, the likelihood is that you'll pick up that pronunciation too and speak it in the same manner.

When you frequently repeat a certain behavioral pattern, that behavior etches itself in your neural pathways. Over time, that behavior becomes **instinctive**. You slowly begin to maintain that habit and even form new ones using that habit as a basis. If you struggle with breaking or changing a certain habit, it is not because you have a weak will; it is because you have not gained complete insight into the behavior or activity you are trying to modify. You do not know **what** triggers that behavior, **how** it affects you, and exactly **why** you keep on doing it.

To break an old habit and form a new one, the very first thing we must do is understand the **Habit Loop.** A Habit loop is a cycle of three steps that help you understand the habit formation system.

The best definition of the Habit Loop is in Charles Duhigg's book *"The Power of Habit: Why We Do What We Do in Life and Business"*. The Habit Loop consists of the

3R's: the **reminder/cue/trigger**, **routine**, and **reward** associated with a habit.

Reminder, Routine, Reward

The **reminder** or **cue** is the activity or event that prompts you to indulge in a certain habit and continue a routine. The **reward** is the emotional or physical gain you enjoy from performing a certain habit. For instance, if you habitually go for a walk at 6am, the moment your 6am alarm rings, the alarm is the **cue** that you should go for a walk, which is the routine you practice daily. You continue with this practice because it helps you stay healthy, which is the **reward** you enjoy from continuously practicing this behavior.

Every habit follows this pattern. The **reminder** is followed by a **routine**, which, in turn, provides you with a certain **reward**. To let go of a habit or to build a new one, you **must** exert absolute control over this loop.

Here is how to do so:

Observe Your Behavior

First, observe a certain behavior you would like to change and analyze it in **detail**. This will help you understand the routine well.

Know the Rewards It Offers You

Next, assess the rewards associated with that habit so you can know why you keep performing it. Does it help you reduce stress? Is it a good way to kill boredom? Does it help you stay fit? Does it make you happy? The reward is a big part of why you practice a specific habit; therefore, understanding the reward helps you know yourself and the way you function.

Identify Its Triggers

To rewrite a habit, you **must** become **conscious** of what sets it off. Each habit you have follows one or more triggers. If you go straight to the washroom to wash your face whenever you wake up, waking up is your **trigger** to wash your face. If you check your email whenever you sit at your desk, sitting at the desk is likely the **cue** that prompts you to check your email.

To break a habit, you must **isolate and change** the cue. If you do not change the cue, breaking that habit will not be easy or possible because the cue pulls you towards the routine.

Find A Substitute That Offers the Same Reward

Finally, you must look for a replacement for the habit you want to break/substitute. Unless you substitute one habit with another one that offers you a similar reward, you will not let go of the bad habit. Because you will miss the reward, you will have a strong compulsion to indulge in that habit.

To ensure this does not happen, find a healthy alternative that provides you with the same or similar reward. This helps you live a better life and enjoy that reward at the same time. In addition, it simplifies the entire habit formation process.

You must build a strategized and detailed plan that will allow you to ease into the new habit and slowly, yet surely, let go of the old one. You also must stay conscious of your triggers. This will give you greater insight on when they occur, which will allow you to use them to trigger the new behavior instead.

Importantly, keep **repeating** that behavior and **reward** yourself when you do it; this will help you solidify the new habit. For instance, if you habitually watch television as you have your meal, something that causes you to binge watch shows for hours, become consciously aware of yourself as you eat. Instead of eating in front of the TV, choose to eat somewhere else so you do not give in to the temptation to switch on the television and remain a slave to the screen.

It is the little things, like this, that define the person you are. Little things, like this, that can and will completely change your life. You will never reap the rewards until you act. You will never understand what you can **receive,** until you start **changing** and **acting**. Please, take the first step now. **You will never regret it.**

If you use this process, and I mean **truly** use it, you **can** and **will** effectively overwrite unwanted habits and build desirable ones that will significantly improve your lifestyle. To do that, it is essential that you learn how to distinguish between your healthy and unhealthy habits.

Analyze your behavior, life, and personality in detail and pinpoint all the little to big habits that build your life in general.

Here are some questions to better understand that:

1. When you wake up in the morning, what is the first thing you tell yourself? Are you dreading another day, or are you happy and ready to take on everything and anything life might throw at you?

2. When you're stuck in traffic, do you become angry? Or do you utilize that time for something a little more constructive or positive? I mean... nothing is going to change the fact that you're sitting there? Right?

3. When you're at work or in class, do you tell yourself how much you hate being there? Or do you tell yourself all the things you're going to do and improve so that you **no longer have to be there**?

4. When you're in an argument with a friend or loved one, do you continue raising your voice and adding flame to the fire? Or do you silence yourself, think, and find a way to improve the situation?

After doing this, analyze those habits and consider how they affect you. If a certain habit makes you feel uneasy, contributes to your routine stress, makes you anxious, and deteriorates your emotional or physical well-being or both, this is a **bad habit**. As opposed to this, if a habit helps you become a better person, improves your attitude, and positively influences your life, this is a **good habit**.

After analyzing your many different habits, identify the ones you need to continue practicing, the ones you need to improve upon, and the ones you need to rewrite with better ones.

First, identify **why** a certain behavior became part of your life and **what** prompted you to maintain it until it became a subconscious habit. Next, figure out **why** you need to overwrite that habit, which you can do by truly and deeply understanding its unhealthy influence on your life. When you understand why you need to overwrite a habit, you will feel motivated to put in the effort needed to bring about change.

Once you decide which of your habits you wish to change, start with one and focus on analyzing its **rewards**, **reminders**, and **routine**. Next, find its positive replacement and draw up an implementation plan.

Through this simple process, you can eliminate any habit that negatively influences you and your life. The **key** to building good habits and breaking bad ones is to understand them as deeply as you can; understanding their **rewards**, finding a positive **replacement**, and once you find a positive replacement, actively and consistently practicing it until it becomes a habit.

P.S. Those are just four examples. Four tiny examples of situations that we **all** face. In truth, it is those who react in the more positive manner that acquire true success in every aspect of their life. I don't care what you have to say: especially if you are just going to justify yourself. The world will never conform to you. **You must change yourself**; that is when you will reap all the rewards life has to offer. That is when your most loved and passion-filled dreams will **become your reality.**

What's next?

Now that you know how to do that, you are ready to begin learning and implementing my self-comprised list of over 27 **life changing** habits. If you truly take the time to focus, and go over each habit, and begin to slowly implement them within your life, I can guarantee you that **you will prosper**.

Part 1
Nurture Your Mind

"A healthy outside starts from the inside."-
Robert Urich

This book dives into various parts. Each part focuses on a set of habits that help you improve and invite great pleasures into certain areas of your life. The different habits discussed in each part will further divide into various chapters. This will make it easier for you to understand each habit individually.

The first part of this book focuses greatly on the improvement and sustenance of your mentality. I could not properly express in words how **crucial** this is to one's success. Ask anyone on the face of planet earth that has ever experienced huge success how they did it, and I guarantee their answer will emphasize the importance of solely one thing: their **mindset**. They will tell you with strong conviction, beside all other factors, that their

mindset is what not only allowed them, but pushed them towards achieving every single little thing they were ever able to achieve. All it takes is the will power to turn the switch: **can you do it?**

So, if you want to change your life, continue reading this book. If you want to learn how to switch your mindset with ease, and live the life you have always dreamed of living, continue reading this book. If you want to get the most out of your day, and squeeze every little drop of opportunity out of life, **continue reading this book.**

Chapter 1

The Power of Your Mentality

"Happiness depends on your mindset and attitude."
— *Roy T. Bennett*

✦

An old proverb states: "As a man thinketh, so is he."

Without a doubt, this statement is of sincere truth. Our thoughts and beliefs serve as the invisible forces which attract all situations and experiences into our life. If we nurture positive beliefs, and sustain a healthy mentality, it is likely we will experience an abundance of happiness, health, and prosperity. Similarly, if we nurture an unhealthy mentality, we will solely attract into our life things comprised of negativity and unhappiness. Therefore, the **form** of mentality that we nurture determines our life's overall course and direction; it determines our **destiny**.

First, to truly understand this, it is crucial that you comprehend how your **thoughts** and **beliefs** work together in **physically** creating your reality.

"Your beliefs become your thoughts, your thoughts become your words, your words become your actions, your actions become your habits, your habits become your values, and your values become your destiny." – Mahatma Ghandi

Sincerely, I could not express this in any better or improved fashion. Ghandi hit it on the spot. Your beliefs become your thoughts, and through the process of manifestation, they are created and implemented **physically** into your life.

Since this is a topic all on its own, I urge you to read my next book: (Coming soon!)

Your mentality consists of the set of beliefs and ideologies you nurture that make you think, feel, behave, and act a certain way. If you nurture beliefs that make you feel unconfident, inadequate, and unhappy, every likelihood is that your thoughts will attract those things and experiences into your life.

This happens because negative emotions program your mind to behave a certain way and act in a restricted manner. For instance, if you are walking on the road and see a dog running towards you, you will register the emotion of **fear**, a negative emotion, and you will begin to run away from the dog. You associate that emotion with running away and the moment you register that emotion, you take action. That negative emotion restricted your mind and made you act a certain way even though different options were available to you. Because you do not **want** to see any other options, you will not be able to: even if they are right in front of you.

This is a clear indication that negative emotions cause you to negate your thoughts, narrowing your perspective or way of thinking. You stay focused on only one option, which is why you invite **similar**

experiences. Therefore, if you have been stuck in a period of sorrow, angriness, or unhappiness, your negative perspective will continuously cause situations which will make you feel similar emotions.

As opposed to this, nurturing positive emotions makes you think positive, which helps you explore more options. In fact, a groundbreaking research study by Barbara Fredrickson shows that those who nurture a positive mentality have a frame of mind that allows them to explore different options and create new opportunities: one's that their negative mindset would have restricted them from.

At the most basic level, positive thoughts broaden your horizon and give you hope that you can do amazing things. When you tell yourself that nothing can limit your potential, how you can be better, and how good things will happen to you, you will start to believe these things. Your subconscious will accept these beliefs and use them to shape a "growth" mindset that shall invite those sorts of things into your life. You will act on the belief that you are unlimited, and you will create something truly outstanding and impactful. You will act on the belief that you can be better, and you will never stop striving to improve yourself. You will believe that not only good, but **GREAT** things could happen to you, and if you **truly** believe it, they will! Once these things become your beliefs, they will be transformed and altered into your thoughts. From this, your **mind** will change, **you** will change, and your **world** will change.

When you are strong and positive, you do not back out of challenges. Instead of succumbing to obstacles, you boldly face them and learn from them; this helps you grow. Moreover, you are not scared of pursuing your dreams or setting bigger goals; this invites prosperity and abundance into your life. That's not all; you begin to **trust** yourself, and I cannot begin to emphasize the importance of that. You start to dig deeper into your personality, and you begin to genuinely discover your true potential: your **unlimited** potential. These changes make you a better person and improve your emotional well-being.

Naturally, when you are mentally healthy, even your health starts to perk up too. To live a good life characterized by good health, wealth, love, and happiness, the first thing you must do is work on your **mindset**.

Habit 1
Build Successful Beliefs

"There is no black-and-white situation. It's all part of life. Highs, lows, middles." – Van Morrison

If you always see things from a negative perspective, it is because you have developed the **habit of doing so**. Since this habit has taken root in your subconscious, it is now quite challenging to get rid of it. Nonetheless, challenging has never meant impossible. For you are the **creator** of your destiny. And for you, **nothing is impossible**.

The right way to let go of a negative mentality is through slowly building the habit of developing strong beliefs that help you frame situations in a more optimistic outlook. To do that, you first need to gain insight into your negative thoughts and explore them so you can determine their meaning and source. This helps you know why you developed those thoughts, and whether they are genuine, or not.

A great way to gain a deeper insight into your thought process is to learn how to calm your racing mind and focus on your thoughts by practicing meditation. This is an extremely important and healthy habit to develop to improve your mentality, but since this is a bigger subject altogether, we shall discuss it in the next chapter.

For now, your task is to understand your negative mindset and slowly develop beliefs that help you become more optimistic.

To do that, implement the following plan:

1 First, choose a time of day when you are free and can devote about 10 or more minutes to yourself.

2 When you have those uninterrupted 10 minutes, take your journal, sit somewhere quiet, and think of any limiting or negative belief that upsets you.

3 Write down that belief and then question its authenticity. Does that belief apply to every situation? Do you have any proof proving otherwise? Have others told you that thing? For instance, if one of your belief states, "I am a failure," rummage through your memory in search of evidence that proves or disproves this belief.

4 Once you learn to question your belief and ask the right questions, your mind will start seeking answers. Your mind answers questions depending on how you ask those questions. If you ask yourself "Am I a failure," your mind will show you instances that prove you are. However, if you ask it questions like "Have I done anything that proves I am not a failure?" You will start to think of many instances that show you are indeed a hardworking person.

5 Next, reply to that belief in a more positive tone. If a belief states, "I didn't do that chore correctly so I'll be terrible at it," change it to "So what if I made a few mistakes in the start. If I stay persistent and put in my best effort, I'll definitely be better at it." Similarly, talk to yourself in this manner keeping your beliefs in consideration and change the connotation of all your beliefs.

6 Do this for 10 minutes and by the time you complete the exercise, you will feel a lot more positive than you did before. You must engage in this exercise every day and whenever you do, treat yourself to a nice meal, get yourself a little present, or do something that makes you happy: always remember to **reward** yourself. This positively reinforces this healthy practice, helps you stick to it, which in turn helps you make it a subconscious habit.

The thing is: you cannot go far in life if you consistently put yourself down. But if you constantly nurture the habit of staying positive, you can bet that you will see yourself from a different perspective, and you will begin to make subconscious decisions that will set you up for the level of success you desire to achieve.

With the passage of time, you will learn to talk to yourself in a positive manner, which will help you shun your inner critic, the negative inner voice that chides you. This will help you counter all the unhealthy beliefs that poison your life and self-belief.

Tip: In the beginning, you will notice that you catch yourself thinking negatively of different situations. Don't critic yourself when you do; simply be **conscious** of this and rephrase your thoughts with positive ones.

Habit 2
Affirm and Believe

"Belief consists in accepting the affirmations of the soul; unbelief, in denying them."
— Ralph Waldo Emerson

Affirmations are phrases and statements you repeatedly say to yourself to speak a certain belief into your life. These self-proclaimed suggestions can be neutral, positive, or negative, and when you frequently say them to yourself, your subconscious begins to accept them as your own. Once your subconscious mind accepts something, the suggestion imbeds itself into your neural pathway and begins shaping your thinking. Affirmations work in a similar manner as your thoughts: **they influence your subconscious mind to shape your beliefs.**

This means that if you frequently say positive things to yourself and tell yourself you can achieve something, you will eventually start to **genuinely** believe it. These positive thoughts will attract great opportunities and experiences towards you, and will allow you to truly prosper and succeed.

A study discussed in the Proceedings of the National Academy of Science examined the effects of positive affirmations on the VMPFC (ventromedial prefrontal cortex) region of the participants' brain. VMPFC is the part of your brain related to self-relevance, which associates with your **self-esteem**, **self-image**, and **self-confidence**.

Researchers divided participants into two groups: a control group that received positive affirmations right before brain scans, and another group that received positive affirmations a little while before the scanning began.

The results of the study clearly showed that the group that received positive affirmations a little while before the scans showed higher levels of activity in the VMPFC region as compared to the control group. This proves that if you ruminate on, and frequently repeat a positive suggestion for a considerably long time, you are likely to experience thoughts and feelings similar to your positive suggestion. Without a doubt, this makes you feel **capable**: a quality that can allow you to achieve profound greatness, and set you on the path to unfathomable levels of success.

If you turn practicing positive affirmations into an everyday habit, you will strengthen your self-belief, develop an attitude that is friendly to the pursuit of your dreams, and build an empowered life. You will stop settling for the mediocre, and instead settle for nothing less than what adds actual value to your life. This will ultimately help you cultivate the life of your **dreams**.

Next...

Now that you understand the power of affirmations, here is what you need to do to practice them regularly:

1 Think of anything you want to change in yourself, any area you want to improve at, or any goal you want to achieve.

2 Write down that thing or goal and then build a positive and present-oriented affirmation around it. Positive here means your affirmation should not include words that have a negative connotation; words such as 'not, never, and 'cannot.' Your subconscious does not recognize the word "not". When you use the phrase in an affirmation, the mind changes the suggestion accordingly. For instance, if you said, "I am not going to be sad," your subconscious mind will change the affirmation to "I am going to be sad." Rather than using negative words in your suggestions**, focus on positive words**. If you wish to be happy, say, "I am happy." Further, the affirmation must be present-focused which means it should make you feel as if you have already achieved your intention. For instance, to attract abundance into your life, say, "I am enjoying great abundance in my life" instead of saying "I want to live a life full of abundance." When you say the latter or any affirmation focused on the future, an affirmation such as "I am going to work hard" or "I am going to be successful," your thoughts will focus on the future and your present will remain devoid of that blessing or goal. As you create affirmations, create positive and present-oriented affirmations.

3 Keep your affirmation as clear and concise as possible. An affirmation of 20 to 30 words is ok, but it is best to keep your affirmation about seven to ten words long. Shorter affirmations are easier to speak, recall, and you can easily repeat them.

4 After crafting your affirmation, write it down in your journal and chant it aloud for about 10 to 20 minutes. To improve its effectiveness, write down the affirmation as you speak it.

5 Speak each word loudly and clearly. Emphasize important words in the affirmation. If an affirmation reads "I breathe in confidence and exhale stress," then emphasize **breathe in**, **confidence**, **exhale**, and **stress**.

6 Feel what you say. If you say, "I am happy," actually smile and inject your maximum belief into the suggestion. The more you believe what you say, the stronger it will affect your mind; when you truly believe something, you become ready act upon that belief. To understand this effect, say "I am happy" twice. In the first instance, say it half-heartedly, then repeat the same statement with complete belief, and as you do it, put a big grin on your face. Compare the feelings you experience the second time with those you experience the first time. You will notice a remarkable difference in how you feel now. You will truly start to feel good and happy inside. **This is the power of belief**.

7 Truly visualize yourself achieving the goal you just set. If you are saying, "I am happy," imagine yourself being the happiest person in the world and feeling that the whole world belongs to you. If you are saying, "I am successful and wealthy," envision being the most prosperous person in the world and living a life filled with nothing other than success and abundance. Live each moment of your visualization and you will start to feel what you say. The practice of combining belief and positive affirmations and then visualizing them turns the affirmation into an incantation. Incantations are a practice Tony Robbins, world-renowned self-help author and coach, swears by. An incantation is simply an empowering suggestion you give to yourself to improve your mentality.

8 Keep practicing this for 10 to 20 minutes or more. For best results, do it twice a day.

9 For even better results, do it once immediately after waking up and then before going to bed. When you say empowering things to yourself when you rise, you set a positive basis for your day. Secondly, by repeating those or similar suggestions before going to bed, you give yourself positive mental food to linger in your mind while you sleep. This will place your mind in a certain state, allowing you to wake up in the mood your suggestion promotes.

Try this practice for a week and the results will amaze you. They will not only put you and cause you to remain in awe, but they will also motivate you to stick to the practice for good.

As you work on improving your mentality for the better, make way for another great habit in your life: **meditation**. This practice helps you gain complete insight into why you behave a certain way and why you support a negative mindset. This allows you to know yourself better and gradually let go of everything that holds you back. As a result, it becomes easier to let go of past resentments and grudges and become more forgiving and thankful. That's not all; meditation can help you to improve your focus, become more productive and even a lot healthier: all of which are important ingredients for success.

Chapter 2

Silence Your Racing Mind

"The punishment of every disordered mind is its own disorder."
— Augustine of Hippo

Note: Profound success comes with responsibility; if you don't know how to calm yourself and handle the pressure that comes with success, you are likely to suffer the harsh consequences of living a life filled with stress. Well, if you cannot manage stress and anxiety, depression might be one thing you'll have to battle with as well.

Experiencing normal amounts of nervousness, stress, and agitation in stressful and upsetting situations is perfectly fine. After all, these emotions are responses activated by the fight and flight center in our body and are there to help us cope with stressful situations.

However, when these emotions begin to disturb you more often, you begin to fall victim to chronic anxiety. This keeps you stressed and frustrated all the time, and further makes it difficult to supply your mind with the constant stream of positivity you need.

To make sure you develop the right mindset, you need to stabilize these issues. This is precisely where meditation comes in handy. Moreover, to develop the right mentality, you also need to know why you think and behave a certain way. Meditation is the perfect practice for this. Before going deeper into the benefits of meditation, let us learn more about what meditation is as well as what it entails.

What is Meditation?

Meditation is a practice that, for thousands of years, has been helping people live better lives. This practice induces a sense of awareness by making you **conscious** of what is going on inside and outside of you. If this sounds confusing, here is an elaborate example.

Imagine that you and your spouse are happily celebrating your anniversary or birthday. Amidst the celebration, you get a call saying you did not land that job you were hoping to get. This upsets you a little. You try to get back into the party mood but somehow, your mind keeps going back to the day of the interview and recalling all the mistakes you think you made.

Instead of letting go of this small setback, you continue wishing how you could turn back time and improve your mistakes so you could have taken this job. This practice frustrates you and before you realize, you are drowning in a pool of sadness, something that keeps you from enjoying the party. This upsets him/her too, and you get into a tiff.

This happened only because you did not control your thoughts or how they affected you; you gave them permission to take control of your mind, giving them full control of yourself, which, in-turn, ruined your entire day. Had you been aware of your thinking pattern, how one tiny thought can lead to a plethora of thoughts that can sabotage your well-being, you would have nipped negative thoughts at the bud and changed them into something positive. Also, had you been more conscious and mindful of the present moment, you would not have let a tiny setback in your past disrupt your future.

This is but one example of how we ruin our present when we do not dwell in it and instead live somewhere in the past or future. Not being mindful affects our daily routine in various ways. Think of the frustration you experience when you are stuck in traffic or how angry you get when you and your partner fail to agree on an issue. Several things happen to you every day where had you behaved sanely and lived in the present, you could have managed the situation in a more positive and efficient manner.

Not being mindful of the present moment and failing to accept is a mistake many of us commit. This mistake births unhealthy thoughts that when held onto, birth unhealthy mindsets. To feel healthy, you need to foster the growth of a healthy mindset. Only after cleansing your mind of unhealthy thoughts can you develop the willpower to develop habits that lead to self-improvement.

If that is your goal, it is important that you learn the art of meditation. How exactly does meditation make you more mindful of your present?

Turn the page and find out.

The Power of Meditation

Meditation saves you by stabilizing your brainwave frequencies. We (humans) have five brainwave states: **Gamma** with *a frequency ranging from 40 to 100Hz*, **beta** with a *frequency ranging from 12 to 40Hz*, **alpha** with a *frequency between 8 to 12Hz*, **theta** with a *frequency ranging from 4 to 8Hz*, and **Delta** with a *frequency between 0 to 4Hz*.

Our brain functions in the gamma and beta state. While these states are important to think, stay alert, and make decisions, when our brain constantly functions in these states, it becomes difficult for us to stay calm and think rationally. We then experience the **'racing mind.'**

Meditation helps you unwind. It does so by stabilizing these brainwave states, and by shifting your mind from the beta state to the alpha or even theta state whenever you want.

By helping you focus on one thing at a time, and dig deeper into your mind, meditation instills in you the awareness you need to understand your thoughts and quickly calm down your mind when need be. This helps you slow your mind, remain composed, live in the present, and let go of everything that does not benefit you in that moment. Along with this, it allows you to concentrate on placing your focus on the things that are going to bring happiness and positivity in to your life.

When you dwell in the moment, you become more aware of your present blessings; this helps you build the **habit of gratitude**. Not only that, meditation (especially mindful meditation) can help you become more forgiving and kind towards yourself and others. When you let go of the resentment you feel, you become more forgiving, and you prepare yourself to create and nurture **meaningful relationships.**

Meditation also helps you practice self-forgiveness and self-acceptance. When you learn to dismiss thoughts that trigger stressful thinking, let go of all the mistakes you made in the past, and stop being over-concerned about your future, you start to forgive yourself for the mistakes of your past.

This helps you accept yourself wholeheartedly and be at peace with yourself. It allows you to truly improve; when you know yourself better, you identify your shortcomings and become committed to improve them. Naturally, when you witness that improvement, you begin to feel proud of yourself, which alters your **self-loathe**, and converts it to **self-love**. This consequently reduces your stress levels and helps you enjoy a more-fulfilled and content life.

As if that is not enough, meditation improves your creative skills, relationships, resilience, decision-making, and problem-solving skills. Because this practice is incredibly brilliant, meditation is one of the 27 life-changing habits you should practice to bring in health, happiness, and prosperity.

How to Meditate

There are different ways to practice meditation. Here, we shall discuss the simplest form of meditation that helps you calm a racing mind, understand your inner-self, and become more conscious: **Mindful breathing meditation**.

Habit 3
Mindful Breathing

"Do every act of your life as though it were the last act of your life." – Marcus Aurelius

Mindful breathing meditation is an amazing practice that induces a state of mindfulness that helps you overcome forgetfulness for good. To achieve this, mindfulness breathing meditation uses your breath. By practicing mindful breathing meditation regularly, you learn to soothe your stressed nerves, better explore your emotions, gain confidence, and improve your thought process.

Here is how you can practice it:

1 Find a calm, quiet, and distraction free meditation spot. It is important that you meditate somewhere peaceful so you stay focused and do not get distracted during the practice. You can meditate anywhere you like such as your garden, bedroom, or a nook in your living room – just ensure the place is distraction free. If you have placed your television or any distracting, noisy appliance there, get rid of it or switch it off so you do not lose focus. Clean the place so it looks tidy and appealing to you. Meditating in a messy, dirty place is difficult because the chaos will constantly distract you.

2 Once your meditation spot is all set, choose a time and duration. The time can be anytime you are free; do not feel the need to tend to other tasks. As for the duration, for starters, meditate for two to five minutes; since meditating for more five minutes may seem too challenging. As you continue practicing, you can increase the duration. However, for now, it is best to stick to under five minutes.

3 When ready to meditate, wear something loose and comfortable. When you are at the meditation spot, sit in any comfortable spot you like. The half lotus, lotus, and seiza poses are the most common poses among meditation practitioners. You can resort to any of these or if they seem difficult, you can sit in an armless, straight back chair, directly on an exercise mat, or even lie down flat. Here is how you can practice the three poses mentioned above.

Half Lotus Pose

For this pose, sit comfortably on the exercise mat and cross your legs. Slightly lift one foot and leg, and place the foot on the opposite thigh. If you wish to lift the left leg, put the left foot on the right thigh or vice versa. Maintain this pose throughout the practice but if it becomes difficult to sit in it for long, you can change the poses whenever you feel uncomfortable.

Full Lotus Pose

This is an extremely stable pose but a slightly challenging one to practice. To practice it, cross both legs and put both feet on opposite thighs.

Seiza Pose

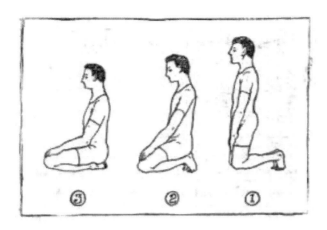

This pose is common in meditation sessions. To practice it, kneel on the exercise mat and then sit upright with your legs underneath you. Now place your feet on the floor behind you in a manner that the toes touch the floor.

Practice any of these poses and when seated comfortably, move to the next step.

4 Now think of any memory, thought, or person that calms you down. Think of your vacation in Mauritius, Bali, Hawaii etc. holding your baby for the first time, or lying on your bed quietly and peacefully.

5 Once you notice yourself becoming calmer, close your eyes, slowly gather your attention, and focus on your breath.

6 Your goal now is to stay with your breath as you inhale and exhale; there is no need to lengthen or deepen your breath. With time, your breathing will deepen as you become better at meditation.

7 Breathe through your nose and focus on only your breath and the various sensations it produces in your body.

8 As you inhale, notice how the rims of your nostrils inflate and when you hold your breath, notice how it distends your abdomen. Upon exhalation, notice how relaxed you feel. Remain focused on your breathe.

9 Your thoughts are likely to wander away. For instance, you may start thinking of the food you are supposed to cook for your family or some other chore you must attend. When this happens, just be patient with yourself and say to yourself, *"Thinking has occurred."* You can even utter these words in your head.

Acknowledge that you just wandered off in thought and then without being harsh, gently nudge your attention back to your breath. Tell yourself "It is my breath. I must concentrate." and then calmly start to focus on your breath again.

10 If distractions become frequent, count your breath. Count one full breath – one inhalation and one exhalation – as one and continue doing so until you count to 10. When you do, start from one.

11 Continue doing this all though your set meditation session and soon, concentrating on, and being attentive to your thoughts will become easier.

12 When your meditation time lapses, slowly and gently open your eyes, and then try to see your surroundings with a fresh new perspective. Do not make any big movements just yet; take time to adjust to the real world. Slowly, make tiny body movements and once you feel ready to get up and attend to your routine chores, leave your meditation spot.

Stick to this practice. It may take you a couple of days or even a few weeks to focus just on your breath for a good five minutes but if you are patient with yourself, you will definitely get there. You will not experience a huge difference in how you feel in the start, but as you progress and become better at concentrating on your breath, you will find a sense of peace building and settling within you.

Once you get better at that, slowly prolong your meditation duration and take it to 10 minutes, 15, and so on until you can easily meditate for about half an hour or more. As you become better at meditation, start to explore your thoughts so you can better comprehend the art of truly understanding yourself.

Habit 4

Think About Your Thoughts

"Drink your tea slowly and reverently, as if it is the axis on which the world earth revolves – slowly, evenly, without rushing toward the future; live the actual moment. Only this moment is life." – Thich Nhat Hanh

To understand your thoughts, start your meditation sessions by focusing on your breath. Once you feel calmer and have focused on your breath for a few minutes, let your mind loose. Earlier, you had to focus on just your breath so your mind did not wander off in to thought. Here, we have lifted that restriction and **you are free to think whatever you want**.

Carefully observe a thought as it enters your mind without labeling it as good or bad, negative or positive, healthy or unhealthy. If you spot a certain thought that makes you feel strongly about something and one that affects your life in a certain way, hold on to it and try to explore it.

Here is what you should do:

1 If a thought suggests, "I have never accomplished my goals; no wonder no one in my social circle respects me," perceive this thought for what it is: a mere thought.

2 Do not label it a negative or positive thought. Meditation teaches you to perceive everything for what it is: a feeling as a feeling, a thought as a thought, and an emotion as an emotion. This is how you learn to detach yourself from negative or unhealthy emotions and thoughts and give them undue importance. If you feel that people do not respect you because you have not accomplished anything worthwhile, explore this thought and seek to understand it. Is it because you have not fulfilled your goals or are you over-exaggerating a criticism someone threw at you? The more you explore a certain thought, the better you will understand the root cause of your anxiety-triggering thoughts and the faster you shall get to the root of the problem.

3Write down your findings in a journal and then go through them repeatedly; this will help you know yourself better.

4 Practice this every day and you will find out what your thoughts really mean. You will learn to dissociate from stress-activating thoughts and feelings and will start identifying the issues that make it difficult to achieve your goals.

With time, you will start becoming calmer and happier. As you become better at analyzing your thoughts, incorporate mindfulness meditation into everything you do. This habit is one you need to nurture to develop a healthy mind/mindset.

Don't Lose Sight

Next, what you must do is gradually make meditation a constant part of your life. At its core, meditation means to be aware of everything that happens inside and outside of you. Making meditation a part of your life means you should stay conscious of all that is occurring within your mind 24/7.

Stress and anxiety infect us because our thoughts are elsewhere as we perform routine chores. While doing laundry, we are not involved in it; while cooking, our thoughts are off wandering; while doing office work, we are busy thinking of how to manage our household expenses. In short, we are never truly present in the moment, which gives **normal** stress a chance to turn **chronic**.

To mitigate stress and gradually overcome it, you need to build the habit of meditating while doing your routine chores.

Here is how you can do that:

1 Whenever you start an activity, do it with full attention, and stay present in it every moment. If you are eating food, take each bite slowly and chew it with full attention. Enjoy its taste and aroma and if a distracting thought pops up, chew even slower so you remain focused on the act and do it mindfully.

2 Be wholeheartedly and completely present in everything you do – from eating, to showering, to doing laundry, to doing work at your office, and so on. When you behave this way, you will stay in charge of your thoughts at all times, and whenever something upsetting pops up, you will identify it. Once you pinpoint a thought that could trigger frustration or an undesirable emotion, you will work on it right on time and figure out its cause before it wreaks your mind.

3 When you do this, you will always stay conscious of yourself. Not only will you learn to let go of stress, you will also learn how to enjoy everything you do. For instance, if you are stuck in traffic, instead of losing your temper, you will use that opportunity to listen to music or spend some alone time.

Why?

This strategy helps you develop many good habits and break several bad ones. Building and breaking habits requires that you identify your **reminders**, know a habit's **routine**, and understand its **rewards**. When you cannot maintain a state of consciousness, doing this becomes challenging. However, by becoming mindful, you easily know what triggers a certain bad habit and what encourages you to continue practicing it. Moreover, when you start developing a good habit, you can keep yourself invigorated by drilling healthy suggestions into your mind.

If you stick to these practices for 60 days or so, they will turn into habits and will shape your life positively. By nurturing the habit of doing everything you do mindfully (including working, talking, listening, responding to emails etc.), you will start noticing just how productive and likeable you become. All that will set you on an express path to massive success in everything you do.

To foster a strong and healthy state of mind, another thing you need to do is forgive yourself and those around you. The next chapter discusses this in detail.

Chapter 3
Forgiveness

"Darkness cannot drive out darkness, only light can do that. Hate cannot drive out hate, only love can do that." – Martin Luther King, Jr.

To many of us, forgiveness, whether it is forgiving those close to us or ourselves, does not come easy. Letting go of the hurt someone caused you and forgiving that person after he or she has wronged you is not as simple as it sounds. How can you compel your heart to be merciful? How can you just let go of all the anger and hate, and truly forgive?

Moreover, forgiving yourself could be just as difficult. Undoubtedly, your past is full of mistakes, and the many setbacks you experience make you feel unworthy and unhappy. When you lowly regard yourself, you will not value yourself. This will cause you to be harsh on yourself whenever you err and falter. Even worse, you will not believe in yourself. You will not supply yourself with the support you need to become the impactful, powerful, and significant person you can truly be. You must learn to forgive yourself; from there, you will let go of what was, and focus on **what can be.**

Although meditation and nurturing a positive mindset allow you to experience peace and calmness of the mind, only when you begin to truly forgive yourself and others can you gain a true sense of **complete inner-peace**.

Here are the different benefits you will enjoy by building the habit of forgiveness.

The Powerful Effects of Forgiveness

If you are one of the few that can truly harness the power of forgiveness, your life will be whatever you want it to be. Although you may not genuinely realize it now, I can guarantee its effects will become apparent quickly. The power of forgiveness will positively impact almost all aspects of your life. Here a few examples.

Saves You Time and Energy

When was the last time you were truly furious about something or someone? Recall that time, and think of how you felt. Were you seething with rage? Did you boil up and create a big scene? Did you waste a lot of time quarrelling with someone to prove your point? Did that entire scenario exhaust you? Did it leave you feeling sad for days, affect your productivity at work, your relationships at home and affect you in many other ways? If yes, then you have experienced the utter horribleness of what it is to be angry and unforgiving. Not only does it completely drain your energy, but it absolutely **wastes your time**; time that you could be using to improve and take a step forward, instead of one backwards. If you want to reach massive success in everything you do, remember this.

Practicing forgiveness will help you save time and energy. When you forgive someone immediately after he or she hurts you, you decommission the resentment factory inside you, which allows you to let go of strong negative emotions. This helps you use your time and energy to complete productive and self-constructive tasks.

At the same time, self-forgiveness ensures that you do not spend too much time loathing and hating the things you have done in the past; which will allow you to learn from all your mistakes, take them in to sincere consideration, and improve your acts in the future. Only this way will you change **yourself**, and change your **life**.

Forgiveness Means You Win

By allowing the person who has wronged you to swarm your everyday thoughts, and control your underlying emotions, you are literally allowing them to walk free with your happiness in their hands. You are giving them the opportunity to strip you of your positive emotions, and ruin your entire day, week, or month. Do not let this happen. Control yourself, control your life!

By simply speaking the words "I forgive you," and letting all of it go, you are the ultimate winner. You are reclaiming your happiness, and therefore a piece of your life.

Become the Boss of Your Life

Unleashing your temper, even if you are doing so occasionally, often births anger issues that hand over control to your emotions. This makes you behave irrationally and surrender control of your life. It can be very challenging to be successful if you have serious anger issues; no one wants to be around you to support whatever it is you are pursuing because of your regular anger outbursts.

By letting the other person or situation take the wheel of your thoughts and emotions, you surrender control of your own life. Forgiveness is the tool which allows you to regain control of that wheel. It will give you the opportunity to take charge of all your decisions, and live a beautiful life consisting of nothing other than health, wealth, love and happiness.

New Doors Will Open

Since you have completely freed yourself of the undermining power of negative thought, energy, and lack of control of your own happiness, you will be surprised to witness just how many new opportunities will begin to pop-up in to your life. But, it is not that they were created from thin air, it is that you have freed space in your mind and have regained control of your positive mentality, allowing you to truly think and notice all opportunities around you.

Even if you are unable to physically say the words "I forgive you" to the person, mentally say them to yourself. Alone, this will allow you to free yourself from negative constraint, and experience life in a more positive, and progressive manner.

It is important to find a healthy and positive balance in your life. Carrying around old baggage from someone who has wronged you is not helping you maintain that balance. Clear the space in your head and look forward to new and exciting opportunities, and most importantly, happiness.

Undoubtedly, it is clear to see that forgiveness is a crucial factor when it comes to building a positive mentality. Although this may be one of the most difficult habits to follow, it is truly one of the most important. Therefore, in order to experience greater ease in this, here is a list of guidelines that helped me in the beginning of my mental transformation. I hope it helps you as well.

Habit 5

Nurture the Habit of Forgiveness

"The weak can never forgive. Forgiveness is the attribute of the strong." – Mahatma Gandhi

To nurture and sustain the crucial habit of forgiveness, follow these guidelines:

1 You already know how to stay aware of your emotions and thoughts. Use that skill to acknowledge hatred, offense, or any emotion of that sort the moment it ignites inside you. For instance, if you and your partner just had a fight, and you feel hurt about something he/she said to you, recognize the emotions you feel at that point.

2 At that instant, tell yourself that you are not angry; tell yourself that this is just another emotion you are experiencing and you **can control it**.

3 To avoid giving into frustration, practice deep breathing and then tell yourself "I am calm; I forgive that person." Inject more belief into this affirmation so you can turn it into a strong and powerful incantation.

4 In a few minutes, you will start relaxing. The moment that happens, approach that person and tell him or her that you forgive them and want to patch up. If you feel the person may be too upset to talk right now, approach the person when he or she is in a better mood.

(Since you would have forgiven the person in your heart, you will not feel the anger burn your insides anymore.)

5 Similarly, whenever you make a mistake, do not hold on to that setback. Instead of criticizing yourself, accept your flaw and say, "I forgive myself completely; I'm going to improve myself." This helps you develop a forgiving attitude towards yourself and move on whenever you experience faltering challenges.

Record your feelings and emotions relating to this habit and every other habit you work on in your journal so you can track your performance.

Chapter 4
Gratitude

"As we express our gratitude, we must never forget that the highest appreciation is not to utter words, but to live by them." - John F. Kennedy

The Power of Gratitude

To nurture your mentality, you **must** foster contentment within **yourself** and your **life**. If you fail to do that, you will keep complaining about one thing or another; this will send unhealthy signals to your mind. In addition, you will feel upset when you fail to achieve what you want, and you will not allow yourself the opportunity to build yourself back up, and start again with improvement.

To live a completely empowered and self-determined life, a cultivation of sincere and genuine gratitude is **essential**. Here are the four biggest reasons why developing this habit is important.

Improves Your Emotional Well-being

When you are thankful for all your blessings and feel happy about yourself and your life, you feel good inside, which automatically improves your emotional and psychological state. Additionally, your blessings open you to the realization of how wonderful your life is; shifting your focus and attention away from the undesirable things, and towards the positive ones. This helps you build an optimistic outlook towards life in general.

Create Healthy Relationships

When you are thankful, you appreciate your loved ones and all the efforts they put in to building a happy and positive relationship. This helps you love and respect them more, which consequently strengthens your existing bond. Along with this, cultivating a sense of gratitude will allow you to see past the negative aspects of small moment interactions, and realize the general beauty, profundity, and happiness that is consisted within that relationship.

Moreover, gratitude makes you more likeable; people are generally attracted to those with a good and likeable nature. Hence, it is likely that when you develop the habit of being thankful, you will build many new and healthy relationships. Not only that, but your true gratitude for these relationships will allow you to get the most out of them, and allow them to prosper into genuine, self-nurturing, and happiness-filled relationships.

Become More Resilient

Gratitude shapes your positive mindset; when you become optimistic, you become more hopeful, and life becomes full of possibilities. When you face an obstacle, instead of backing down, you stand up to it and boldly face it because you know you will find light at the end of the tunnel if you stick to what you believe in.

Another thing gratitude does is that it makes you aware of your blessings; this helps you disregard your obstacles. Instead of viewing them as something monstrous, you perceive them as routine challenges; this motivates you to find ingenious ways to fight back.

Become Generous

Developing gratitude also makes you sensitive to the needs of others. When you see underprivileged people around you, you become empathetic towards them and become more aware of their sufferings. This helps you realize how blessed you are and consequently makes you more caring towards others.

You learn to help others, take care of their needs, and become more compassionate towards them. Your generosity attracts more happiness, serenity, and love into your life.

Gratitude is indeed a wonderful attitude to develop and one that improves every area of your life.

Due to our human nature, practicing gratitude 24/7 can seem almost impossible. I assure you, though, it is not. If you believe me, you will experience its many **rewards**. Here are a few tips on how to implement gratitude in to your life.

Habit 6

Build the Habit of Gratitude

"Gratitude can transform common days into thanksgivings, turn routine jobs into joy, and change ordinary opportunities into blessings." - William Arthur Ward

These strategies will help you become more thankful and appreciative of your life:

1 Every day when you wake up or before going to bed, take note of any three blessings in your life and contemplate on their importance. These can be anything from having a good job, to loving friends, to wearing good clothes. Remember to take note of any little to big blessings in your life that adds value, convenience, comfort, happiness, and any sort of positivity to your life. You could make this practice a morning or nighttime ritual, or even both.

2 Create a list of your strengths and qualities and use them to feel proud of yourself. Tell yourself how thankful you are to the universe for these qualities.

3 Build affirmations centered on gratitude such as "I am happy with my life," and chant them regularly so you become more appreciative of your blessings.

4 Soon, you will learn to acknowledge different acts of kindness others do for you. The moment you spot someone being nice to you, you will approach that person and say a few kind words of gratitude. This will make that person's day and increase your happiness too.

Implement these exercises and do so every day. The more you practice them, the sooner they will turn into habits. Focus on how good you feel as you work on these exercises and write down your feelings. Going through your written feelings encourages you to engage in positive practices regularly.

In addition to doing this, bring freshness to your life by doing something new and creative regularly. This gives you a fresh perspective of things, and gives way for great opportunity.

Chapter 5
Try Something New

"We keep moving forward, opening new doors, and doing new things, because we're curious and curiosity keeps leading us down new paths." – Walt Disney

Remember

You have the power to change the world; but you can only do so by changing yourself first.

Is your current life monotonous? Do you feel as if your life has nothing new to offer? Does this annoy you or turn you into a chronic complainer? If yes, it is because you have stopped trying new things. You are so used to doing the same things that it is almost like you are a robot. Let me ask you something: if you never give yourself the chance to try new things, how can expect your life to change? How can you expect your life to go in a different direction than the one it is currently going in if you don't change any of your **thoughts**, **actions**, or **behaviors**? Seriously, How? Don't even bother giving an answer to that, because I know there is none. You must know that you are the **creator** of your own destiny. If you want to remain stuck in a rut, then by all means do so. If you want to change yourself and your life for the better, to experience new and wonderful things, to be truly happy, than **make change**. If you expect your life to just change while you're lying in bed or sitting on the couch, you are sadly mistaken, and in for a rude awakening.

A healthy mindset is one that is stimulated and energized. One that remains optimistic, and seeks opportunity in all its ventures. Good news: doing new things is the best way to achieve this type of mind.

Here are five great habits that will help you broaden your horizons and build new opportunities to live an exciting and enjoyable life.

Habit 7

Try Something New Every Day

"I realized something on the ride. I realized if I wait until I'm not scared to try new things, then I'll never get to try them at all."
— Marie Sexton

Get into the habit of doing something completely new every day. Each day, embark on a tiny or big new adventure and do something completely different from the ordinary. Do not worry; this need not be something too adventurous such as paragliding. You can bring in those activities later when your adventurous spirit is thriving.

In the start, just do simple and new things such as eating at a different café for lunch each day, taking a new route to work, or listening to a different genre of music. This practice brings a lot of freshness into your life and helps you explore yourself better.

Here are some ideas for you:

1. Build a new ritual such as a reading a book before going to bed

2. Listen to a new genre of music

3. Cook different types of food

4. Go out and explore where you live; explore your environment

As you become comfortable with the idea of trying new things, try more adventurous activities and practices such as bungee jumping, skydiving, and cliff jumping. Moreover, you can also learn new skills such as pottery, painting, or playing a musical instrument. This broadens your skill set and adds a lot of fun into your life.

Do something new and out of your comfort zone every day, and then slowly work your way up to more exciting activities. This will help you become more adventurous; it will also add freshness to your everyday life.

Why?

By developing a mindset of doing new things regularly, you are unlikely to find it extremely difficult to try new things that propel you to success. In particular, you can nurture the habit of doing something new that pertains to the things you want to achieve in life. This will ultimately get you closer to the success you've always envisioned to attain.

To make the above habit work for you with even greater effectiveness, you can combine it with the habit of approaching things with curiosity.

Habit 8
Be Curious

"I have no special talent. I am only passionately curious." – Albert Einstein

In addition to trying your hand at new activities, approach things with more curiosity and less caution. If something strange or unexpected happens to you, do not fear it or label it as a negative experience. Instead, perceive it with a curious outlook and try to find any positivity associated with it.

If the selection committee failed to select you for a dance competition, perhaps it is because your purpose in life is to become a singer and not a dancer, or maybe it is because a bigger, better opportunity awaits you.

A study conducted by the Michigan State University in October 2013 showed that taking part in activities that stimulate your curiosity and creativity is a great way to improve your cognition. Such activities improve the connectivity and functionality of different areas of your brain and consequently enhance your cognitive function.

To make this practice a habit, add curiosity to the different elements, activities, and areas of your life. If you learn about a new approach to doing something, find out what that technique entails and how it can help you. If someone tells you of a DIY remedy to cure upset stomach, dig deeper into that antidote and find out how helpful it is.

Be curious about everything you cross paths with and learn as much as you can. This increases your knowledge of things, sharpens your cognition, and provides you with more opportunity than you could ever imagine.

By nurturing the habit of being curious and learning everything, you will easily be able to capture new opportunities whenever they present themselves. You won't easily write off ideas just because they seem unfamiliar, but will investigate them before passing judgment. This is a great trait to have as someone who wants to excel in life because there will be many opportunities that come your way as you work towards success. How fast you take on the opportunities will greatly determine whether you 'run with it' or not.

Habit 9

Constantly Overcome Fear

"If you want to conquer fear, don't sit home and think about it. Go out and get busy." –
Dale Carnegie

In addition, get into the habit of habitually overcoming the fear associated with new and challenging ideas or situations. Whenever a challenge knocks on your door, do not shut yourself in out of fear. Instead, gradually welcome the challenge and understand its purpose. Obstacles are not there to put you down; they are there to help you become better. If you learn to approach obstacles as learning opportunities, you will slowly overcome the fear associated with it. Not only this, but you will learn much more than you ever could have being afraid.

Similarly, when you must do something outside your comfort zone, do not perceive it as something impossible; consider it as an experiment. Instead of overthinking things, just do it. Once you engage in challenging or adventurous activities a couple of times, you will build the habit of letting go of fear, which will expose you to new ideas and trains of thought.

Alone, this habit will push you towards the success you never thought was possible.

As you work on overcoming your fears every single day, it is also important that you develop a habit of building on your strengths and past accomplishments.

Habit 10
Build Your Strengths

"Strength does not come from winning. Your struggles develop your strengths. When you go through hardships and decide not to surrender, that is strength." – Arnold Schwarzenegger

We have already stated that to feel good about yourself, one of the things you can do is build a list of your strengths. I hope you created that list, because now you are going to take it out and build on it. Find ways to hone your strengths and turn them into valuable skills. For instance, if you are good at playing guitar, make sure to set aside time each day to improve this craft and level up your skill.

Similarly, tap into your different strengths and develop the habit of doing something that utilizes your skills. Take one strength each day and make a list of different practices that could help you focus on and improve that talent. Try each of those techniques each day and by the end of two weeks, you will have realized many skills you never knew you had, and you will have improved the many you did.

You could work on a new strength each week or each month. After a few months, you will have several skills up your sleeve and will feel very proud of yourself.

Additionally, develop a habit of learning from your accomplishments and using those experiences and lessons in new experiences. If you face a tricky obstacle, rummage through your memories and figure out how you resolved problems in the past and emerged victorious in the end.

Building on your accomplishments and using that knowledge to do well in the present is another good habit that strengthens your mindset and helps you create new strategies that help you resolve issues. By so doing, you can be sure that you will ride on your successes to become even more successful in whatever you do.

For instance, if you are pre-school teacher who deals with little toddlers, you could take lessons from your experiences with your previous class to work on the new one. Taking this example further, if one of your current students has anger issues and throws tantrums, recall a time when you dealt with a similar student a couple of years back and how you encouraged that student to behave nicely. Using lessons from your accomplishments will help you build on your achievements and will even make your present better too.

Remember: keep this in mind every single day. Live your life to the fullest. Because if you don't, it will be empty.

Habit 11

Live Your Life to the Fullest

"Life is a game, play it; Life is a challenge,
Meet it; Life is an opportunity, Capture it."
– Unknown

Every day when you wake up, tell yourself "Today I am going to have the best day ever." Say it a couple of times with an utterly deep and profound conviction. Say it as often and as powerful as you can; begin to truly believe it. Remember this suggestion and feed it to yourself every day. This helps you perceive everything with new found optimism and take interest in everything you do.

This habit helps you live your life to the fullest and see things with a fresh perspective. When you are determined to see past all negativities and obstacles, and you focus on the sincere hope you have for a better future, your day, week, month, and year will experience an over-abundance of significant improvements.

All the habits we have discussed in this first part of the book stimulate your mentality and push you towards realizing your **true** potential. If implemented, they will allow you to become a more positive, self-realized, intellectual, creative, and courageous individual. They will allow you to understand who you truly are, and how large of an impact you can make in this world: if you choose to do so. Not only that, but they will drive you towards levels of success you never even thought were possible.

Now, if you want this, continue reading. If you truly want to be the person you can be, with applied effort, please continue reading, for this book is precisely for you.

Remember, your life is your canvas. Paint it with bright colors, and watch it truly shine.

Part 2

If There Is a Key to Life, It's Happiness

"It is not how much we have, but how much we enjoy, that makes happiness."- Charles Spurgeon

In truth, happiness is about making moments count. With that being said, it could be inferred that making all moments count is the key to living a good and fulfilled life. To understand this more profoundly, let us discuss several aspects of a life consisting of happiness.

Your mindset truly is an important contributor to your happiness, which is why we discussed it in the first part. If your mindset is right, you can achieve health, wealth, love and happiness.

Since you have already learned how to develop a healthy mindset, it is now time to focus on happiness and all the things that help you invite joy, prosperity, and serenity into your life.

Chapter 6

Promote Your Happiness

"Success is not the key to happiness. Happiness is the key to success. If you love what you are doing, you will be successful."
– Albert Schweitzer

Unfortunately, many of us believe that happiness is an offshoot of or by-product of monetary success and you can only be happy if you achieve a certain goal or level of financial success. **This is not true.** In fact, this could not be farther from the truth.

Although happiness is relative and its definition varies from one person to another, associating happiness with the fulfillment of certain things makes happiness a materialistic element, something it is not.

So, what exactly is it to be "truly" happy?

Happiness is being content from within.

True happiness is experiencing true contentment, and a deep and complete sense of peace and fulfillment with who you are, what you do, and what you have done.

To achieve this state, you do not necessarily need to be a millionaire or actualize every goal you set: many underprivileged and even ailing people are happy deep inside because they have educated themselves on how to be happy even when things do not go their way.

In truth, happiness is an art.

The sooner you master it, the sooner you master life.

Habit 12
Be Flexible

"Stay committed to your decisions, but stay flexible in your approach." – Tony Robbins

Most of us constantly remain in the habit of becoming upset when things fail to go as planned. This emanates from our desire to control every little thing in our life because we feel if we can counter stress, we can become happy, or if we can achieve success and make money, we will automatically become happy.

During our pursuit of "happiness", we become controlling. Although we may feel as if this practice helps us, it actually does the complete opposite. To be truly happy, we must build the habit of letting go, which we can do by becoming flexible and adaptable.

Stop being too controlling; no matter how much you try to perfect things, life will always throw something unexpected your way. Understand that inner-happiness, self-realization, and self-reliance are what help you become successful, not control.

If you are happy from within, you will naturally feel less stressed. When you experience less stress, you will think better and feel positive. In turn, this will allow you to approach life with a completely different perspective; one that allows you to remain progressive and hopeful. One that allows you to understand and realize your unlimited potential. One that will never stop pushing you towards achieving all the goals you have set out for yourself. Without a doubt, this is what gives you the ability to alter your life, and turn it into an abundance of successes.

From this day onwards, vow to become less controlling. If your brother is constantly teasing you and does not stop even after telling him several times, become oblivious to the bothersome behavior. The next time he pesters you, give him a big smile and keep doing what you were doing. Your ignorance will certainly put him off and eventually make him stop. Similarly, stop controlling tiny to big things around you and just work on improving yourself. In this case, you must be selfish to be selfless. You must stop worrying about the things going on around you, and focus solely on improving yourself. At that time, you will be able to experience true selflessness; for how could you give, if you don't know how much you have to give?

Habit 13
Smile

"Let us always meet each other with smile, for the smile is the beginning of love." –
Mother Teresa

Smiling truly is an amazing habit that can improve your life in many ways. Firstly, smiling gives you a direct burst of positive emotions right when you need them. When you're experiencing troubles, or stuck in an upsetting situation, throw a smile on your face. Recall all the truly amazing things you have been blessed with in your life, and how they have influenced and molded you into becoming the strong, intellectual, and genuine person you are today. Remind yourself of all the amazing experiences you've had throughout your life, and fill yourself with an intensely motivating excitement for all the ones that have yet to come. Utilize **the power of gratitude** as a tool to drive and intensify your positive emotions. After that, throw the largest grin on your face and allow yourself to

truly feel it. Feel the smile genuinely affect your inner-being, and let your positive emotions course throughout your entire self. If you do this, you will reap the **true** psychological rewards of promoting your happiness.

Additionally, smiling allows you to promote your happiness to those around you. It signals to people that you are a generally positive and optimistic individual: a trait that is extremely uncommon. This characteristic will attract many people into your life, and allow you to create and nurture many meaningful relationships. Once you accomplish this, you will have the whole world with you.

Here are a few strategies to help you make smiling a habit:

1 Upon waking each morning, put a big smile on your face and deliberately grin. Do this for a few seconds and before you realize it, you will start feeling happy – do this every day by setting reminders on your phone.

2 After every 30 to 40 minutes, make a conscious effort to feel happy about something you did and smile. If you were cooking and you made the meal earlier than you expected, say "well done" and smile. If you were exercising and you did a tough routine today, appreciate yourself and smile. This way, you will learn to feel good about everything and smile a lot.

3 Whenever you meet someone, greet him or her with a lovely smile. Do this each time you meet someone even if you see that person many times a day. Also, whenever you thank someone for doing you a favor, give that person the sunniest and genuine smile you can muster.

Habit 14
Pay Attention to Body Language

"What you do speaks so loud that I cannot hear what you say." – Ralph Waldo Emerson

Your body language has a direct impact on your mood and overall well-being. If you have a healthy body language, you are more likely to feel happier and pleasant when compared to those who display an unhealthy body language. A study discussed in the Journal of Behavior Therapy and Experimental Psychiatry proves that.

The researchers asked the participants to walk on treadmill and walk either in a cheerful or glum walking style. While the subjects trudged, and bounced along, the researchers showed them words that elicited sad and happy emotions. Later, researchers asked the participants to remember as many words as possible. The results showed that those who had a happier gait recalled words associated with happiness and those who had a gloomy walking style remembered words associated with sadness.

This proves that a happier and high power body language clearly improves your mood and makes you feel happier. If you want to enjoy these benefits, work on your body language in the following ways:

1 First, correct your posture. Stand upright, broaden your shoulders, and straighten your spine while still maintaining the small curve in your lower back. Lift your head a little and open your hips a little wider. Now open your legs and walk using this posture. Do it a couple of times and set a reminder reminding you to walk in this posture. Soon, you will develop the habit of walking in this manner; this will uplift your mood in general.

2 Secondly, maintain a **high-power** body language. A high-power body language means you must keep your limbs open, maintain direct eye contact when talking to people, and keep your back and head straight instead of slouching and lowering them respectively. According to Amy Cuddy's research, high power poses boost the testosterone levels in your body. Testosterone is a hormone linked with confidence and happiness. When you practice high power body languages frequently, you build a habit of using them regularly and always feel confident and happy.

The truth is: your body language will also influence your odds of becoming even more successful in whatever it is you are pursuing. Why is that so? Well, for starters, portraying confidence in your body language makes other people respect you and take you more seriously. Alone, this can easily place you into the leadership position, which, in turn, makes you seem much more believable. It is easier to persuade people when your body language evokes a feeling of confidence and authority.

Having the right body language equipped when meeting someone new truly can lead the relationship to begin in the right direction.

This will give you greater ease when you begin to...

Chapter 7

Foster Meaningful Relationships

"Truth is everybody is going to hurt you: you just gotta find the ones worth suffering for." – Bob Marley

Your relationships form the essence of your life.

A life devoid of healthy and loving relations is a meaningless life because without loved ones, you have nobody to enjoy success with, share your sadness with, or celebrate your life with.

If your relationships are strained and lifeless, this could be the reason why you stay gloomy and depressed. To be truly happy and delighted about life, it is crucial that you **foster meaningful relationships**.

By doing something as simple as adding emphasis and meaning in every important relationship in your life, you can make your life more valuable and amazing. Before you start improving your relationships, you first need to identify the people in your social circle who positively influence you and make you happy.

Here's how.

Habit 15

Filter Your "Friends"

"You are the average of the five people you spend the most time with." – Jim Rohn

Jim was right: If you closely examine your personality and then look at the five people you hang out with the most, you will notice that you have picked many habits, traits, qualities, and shortcomings of all those five people. That is because when you spend lots of time with someone, that person's behavior starts to influence you in some way whether you realize it or not.

Have you ever noticed how chirpy and cheerful you become after spending a few hours with a highly spirited person or how gloomy you feel when you spend a day with a depressed person? The explanation behind this is that it is in your brain's design to notice and adopt cues from your surrounding environment.

To be happy inside and out, you **must** surround yourself with the right sort of people. You should spend the most time with positive, happy, calm, confident, successful, and honest people who uplift your spirits, encourage you to be better, inspire you to follow your dreams and provide you with healthy criticism that will help you grow.

At the same time, it is also important to distance yourself from naysayers. While healthy criticism is good for you and you need it to become the best you, **naysayers do more than provide healthy criticism: they throw spears of frustration, gloominess, negativity, and jealousy towards you**.

Instead of encouraging you to be good, they constantly bombard you with stories of failure and make you feel incompetent and inadequate. **You do not need** that influence in your life.

To make life beautiful, filter your life of all the unhealthy influences and focus more on those who matter. Let go of **regressive** relationships and maintain **progressive** ones.

To do that, analyze all the people in your social circle: starting with those you hang out with the most. Next, think of how they influence you, and how they truly make you feel about yourself. If that influence is healthy and positive, that person needs to stay in your life. However, if that influence makes you feel terrible about yourself, detach yourself from that person: if not for good then at least until you become strong enough to not allow what people say influence you.

Start slowly distancing yourself from the negative influences in your life and hang around positive ones. Write down how you feel after making this change and within a week, you will notice a remarkable improvement in how you perceive your life. Your outlook towards life will change, which is a fantastic achievement by itself.

Make this practice a consistent habit; constantly analyze how a certain person affects you and then use that to figure out whether to let go of or keep someone in your social contacts.

For instance, if you interact with the new, just-hired marketing manager in your firm and feel that he inspires you, use this as a cue to build a good relationship with him; it is likely that he could help you in many ways.

PS: You cannot be 100% immersed in success if you have people around you that constantly critic your decisions (in a negative way) and put you down. You will soon run out of steam with such people around you. But if you cannot distance yourself from them physically, at least you can do that mentally; just stop telling them what's happening in your life. Look for other things to talk about that don't relate to what it is you are working towards to succeed.

Once you figure out which social contacts to keep and let go of, work on the following habits to improve your relationship with those people.

Habit 16

Network and Connect with Others

"The richest people in the world look for and build networks, everyone else looks for work." – Robert Kiyosaki

Make a conscious effort to **connect** with loved ones and social contacts daily. Without good relationships, not only will your life be completely void of true happiness and fulfillment, but you also won't have that constant stream of love and support that we all truly desire. This support is of vital importance; it will be there to cheer for your when things are going well, and help you bounce back when you stumble upon failure.

Along with this, always place focus on building your list of social contacts, and creating good relationships with each one of them. Although this **may** not make a huge impact on your life now, you will surely notice its effect on your life in the long run.

Whenever you miss a friend or family member, call the person and talk to him or her for a little while. Doing this regularly will reinforce your bond with that person and strengthen your relationship. This habit is one that will benefit you in the end: it will ensure you always stay connected to loved ones who will constantly supply your life with love and happiness.

Moreover, use this habit to **network** more. Networking is a practice that will be of immense benefit to your personal and professional life. From this day onwards, habitually attend professional gatherings and network as much as you can. They will undoubtedly be a strong pillar in your quest towards massive success because you can always get help, inspiration, ideas and other forms of support from your social contacts.

Habit 17

Spend Quality Time with Loved Ones

"At the end of your life, you will never regret not having passed one more test, not winning one more verdict, or not closing one more deal. You will regret time not spent with a husband, a friend, a child, a parent." – Barbara Bush

You absolutely **must** nurture the habit of spending quality time with the people you love. Instead of staying in touch with them through phone calls, text messages, and social media, spend real face-to-face time with them. This will give you the opportunity to actually get to know them better, which will improve your bond.

For instance, each Sunday could be a family day when you take your spouse and kids for a picnic, an amusement park, or any other place where you can and spend maximum time with them. You could hang out with your best friend on Thursdays or any other day that works well for you. Similarly, make several other rituals you stick to on a regular basis so that you never stay away from your loved ones.

How does this help in success? Well, as I stated, success means different things for different people. Nonetheless, without strong support from family and friends, you are likely to feel empty inside. A time spent with your dear ones is one well spent. And if you don't have a good relationship with your loved ones, you are likely to have a very shallow and meaningless relationship with anyone else.

Habit 18
Show Affection

"If you want something to last forever, you treat it differently. You shield it and protect it. You never abuse it. You don't expose it to the elements. You don't make it common or ordinary. If it ever becomes tarnished, you lovingly polish it until it gleams like new. It becomes special because you have made it so, and it grows more beautiful and precious as time goes by." – F. Burton Howard

Spending time with loved ones and social contacts is not enough. You also have to show them your love and care. Quite often, we do not say little things like "I love you" or "You mean a lot to me" to our loved ones. In fact, we often disregard the fact that they may be looking forward to hearing these words from us. Years pass by and when our dear ones bid us goodbye, we start regretting why we did not express our love to them.

To keep loved ones close to you and happy, be more expressive towards them. Instead of being stingy with your words and caring gestures, be more generous when it comes to loving them and showing it.

Get into the habit of showing your affection, love, and care to all those who mean the world to you and those that add color to your seemingly dull life.

How can you do that? Here are some ideas for you:

1 Habitually send loving text messages or emails to your partner, spouse, parents, kids, best friends, and other loved ones once a day or at least once every two days. When you wake up, send a sweet message to your parents letting them know you are thinking of them. In the evening, you could send a voice message or a short video of yourself saying kind things to your loved ones. Do this until doing so becomes a hard to break habit.

2 When you meet your loved ones, do not just shake hands with them. Instead, go the extra mile and give them a nice, warm hug. Hugs are one of the best present in the world; they speak volumes about your love for your dear ones. A simple hug often does wonders – something many words alone cannot do. The next time you meet your best friend, hug him/her hard, and do it whenever you meet him/her after a while. By doing this, you will slowly nurture this good habit.

3 Moreover, get into the habit of giving nice presents to loved ones and not just on birthdays or anniversaries. Regularly giving your loved ones presents is a beautiful habit that fosters your relationships and keeps the spark alive. Presents do not necessarily have to be expensive or grand; simple things can work well too. For instance, on your way back home from work, bring your wife her favorite flowers, or each time you visit your mother, take along her favorite carrot cake. If you do this regularly, you will notice your loved ones showering more affection on you.

Build these habits. To sustain them, notice how much your loved ones enjoy the new you. Their positive feedback and happiness will motivate you to stick to these newfound habits. Another great set of habits that can improve your emotional well-being is to look for the good associated with every situation you experience.

Chapter 8

See the Good in Every Situation

"Discipline your mind to think positively; to see the good in every situation and look at the best side of every event." – Roy Bennett

Why does Roy Bennett advise us to train our minds to see the good associated with every situation? Why does he ask us to disregard the negatives and focus more on the positives?

Well, Bennett does this because when we learn to see the good in every experience, we learn many valuable lessons. Instead of being gloomy, something that happens when we focus on negatives, this practice teaches us to extract positive lessons from worst-case scenarios.

To live a good life, a life that gives you contentment, start focusing on the good linked to every situation. This is only possible when you understand that life is full of obstacles, not a bed of roses. Challenges and difficulties are an integral part of life; they add meaning to your life because if it were not for these challenging obstacles, the happy times would feel stagnant, boring, and flat.

It is the hardships in life that make us value the good times; it is the turmoil that makes us enjoy the fruit we reap after suffering, and it is the darkest of experiences that make us unleash our full potential.

Challenges are not bad and by altering your approach as well as how you perceive them, you can make them better. Instead of seeing the negativities attached to challenges, **look at the positives**. The moment you adopt this outlook, the toughest of obstacles will start appearing positive to you. In fact, you could even start viewing challenges as learning opportunities or opportunities for new business frontiers. Think about it; if you are persistent about success and are success hungry, you will see the challenges you are facing as opportunities where you can teach others or help others to solve similar problems, which of course will translate to you being an authority in that particular aspect.

This practice shall also reduce your routine stress thus allowing you to stay happy every day. If this excites you, here is how you can develop the amazing habit of seeing the good in all situations. Before we discuss that, let us briefly discuss the three basic components that are comprised in **all** situations.

The 3 Basic Components of a Situation

A situation, be it a good, bad, or neutral, has three main elements. Understanding these elements will help you comprehend a situation and if you build the habit of working on these three elements, you can adopt the right attitude and perceive every situation as positive even when everything states otherwise. We shall look at these elements and then discuss how to build the habit of improving these elements.

Attitude

Your attitude is your settled way of feeling or thinking about something. For instance, if you have a positive demeanor, you most likely have a positive attitude towards things and life in general. On the other hand, if you are grumpy, your attitude is likely to be negative, sad, and irritable. If someone says, "What a lovely and bright day it is," you are likely to pinpoint how the sun gives you headaches.

Your attitude is a big contributor to how you perceive different situations, specifically the negative ones. When something positive happens to you, you feel good inside and do not worry about what may happen next. When good things keep happening to you, you are likely to take your blessings for granted, and lose your sense of gratitude and appreciation for them.

As opposed to this, when you suffer, you immediately go into a depressed state and start anticipating all the terrible things that could happen next. This common attitude is one many of us support; it keeps us from seeing the good in situations and from being appreciative of our blessings.

To develop the right attitude, one that allows you to see the positivity in everything, you must work on bettering your attitude. We shall discuss how to do so later in this chapter.

Awareness

Your awareness of the present is another element that shapes your perception of different situations. If you are 100% present in the moment and are aware of what is happening to you and around you in a specific situation, you will perceive a situation for what it is.

Instead of labeling a situation as bad, you will look for the positive and negative aspects associated with the situation and will know that you will get through it despite its severity and huge magnitude.

However, if you are not aware of the moment and are instead forgetful of what is happening to you and the things going on around you, you will miss all the opportunities a certain situation brings.

For instance, if you fail to clinch the post of head of a committee in college, you may be upset; however, if you are fully aware, you will realize that this is actually a good thing – you will have more time to focus on your academics and other activities that require your involvement. Hence, to see the good in every situation, your sense of awareness needs to be **strong** and **powerful**.

Action

Once you perceive a certain situation a certain way, you begin to react. The action taken in relation to that situation is determined by how you perceive it. For instance, when you meet your best friend after a long time, you feel happy because you are aware of his/her presence and on seeing him/her, you feel good inside. You perceive that situation as positive, and you immediately jump to hug that person. Hugging your friend is the action you take in response to that situation.

Similarly, if you experience a negative situation such as seeing a snake in your bathroom, you may run away from it. Running away is your action in response to that fearful situation.

To build the right approach and right way to perceive every situation, you also need to improve your action even as you improve upon the other two elements. To make the most of any situation, you need to act positively and in the right manner.

By pairing the right level of **awareness**, positive **action**, and glass half-full **attitude**, you can be sure that you will be in for lasting success because this is exactly what is required to do so.

Now that you know the three basic elements that make up a situation, let us discuss how to work on, improve, and build these 3 components.

Habit 19

Nurture the Habit of Seeing the Good in Every Situation

"Instead of complaining that the rose bush is full of thorns, be happy the thorn bush has roses." – Proverb

Here is how you can nurture the habit of improving your **attitude**, sense of **awareness**, and **action** related to a situation to extract the good out of it:

1 First, become fully aware of everything you experience moment to moment. If your sense of awareness is high and you dwell in the present, you can see a situation for what it is and slowly work on improving your attitude and action associated with it. If you are absent minded, you will not be aware of the positives associated with a good situation let alone the good in a bad situation. To nurture the habit of being completely aware of each moment as it occurs and passes by, build the <u>habit of practicing meditation</u> while doing your routine chores. This will make you mindful, and the more mindful you become, the more **enhanced** your sense of awareness shall be.

2 As your sense of awareness improves, your attitude associated with different situations will improve too. When you perceive things for what they are and learn to become mindful of your present, you start seeing little blessings you can enjoy each moment. This helps you nurture a more positive attitude that helps you look for the good in every situation. If you lose a client, instead of crying over spilt milk, you will look at the lessons you learnt from that loss and work towards improving your mistakes so you become a better service provider. If you and your partner fight over an issue, instead of letting his/her temper annoy you, you will instead focus on how much he/she loves you and that he/she wants nothing but the best for you. With time, you will build the habit of seeing everything with an optimistic and hopeful attitude.

3 With the first two steps nailed, it is time to work on the habit of improving your action. It is best to move to this habit slow and steady so you do not rush through the process, and instead learn how to act right. To nurture this habit, look at what you learned from a certain situation. What lessons did it teach you? How does it help you become better? Keeping those factors in mind, choose a certain action and then exercise it. Continuing with the example where you lost a certain client, you may realize that your service is not of excellent quality and you create strategies to improve it. This action helps you become a better service provider in your industry, which in turn helps you bag more clients. In the end, your one right action courtesy of your heightened awareness and good attitude will help you enjoy better success.

Implement these practices and consistently work on bettering them so you can convert them into lifelong habits that invite success and happiness towards you from all angles and different directions.

This, in fact, is how you properly squeeze every drop of opportunity out of life.

Chapter 9

Be Resilient: Bounce Back

"Persistence and resilience only come from having been given the chance to work through difficult problems." – Gever Tulley

Resilience is an imperative part of living an empowered life. If you are not resilient, you will not bounce back each time set-backs punch you hard in the gut. When things do not go your way, you are likely to feel upset and if you lack resilience, you can fall into the trap of negative thinking. Without a doubt, I can easily say that anyone who has ever experienced great success in **anything** is resilient. For without this resilience, they would have never had the **ability** and **courage** to take life's punches, and keep moving forward. In fact, they would have been punched once, and remained on the floor in a puddle of pity, negativity, and unhappiness. Therefore, success in life calls for resilience and persistence. So, if you don't have these qualities, continue reading so you can learn how to acquire them. For without them, one will never be able to experience the true and profound **success** one is capable of.

To be truly happy and pave the way for success in your life, you must develop **resilience**: the ability to fight back whenever you encounter an obstacle that knocks you down. You must never settle for the mediocre, and you must always strive for greatness.

Here is how you can build the habit of being resilient.

Habit 20

The 3 Keys of Resilience

"It may sound strange, but many champions are made champions by setbacks." – Bob Richards

To become resilient enough to persevere through any adversity, you need to work on **three key things**: these three things are the three habits you need to develop strength and grit.

Have a Purposeful Goal

Resilience comes easy when you know what you are striving for. To be truly gritty, it is important that you **pursue your goals**. If you do not have any goal, your life will be purposeless. Success will come by chance and you are unlikely to be swayed by anything that comes by. When you lack a sense of purpose, setbacks will easily distract you and you will take your eyes off the prize.

A purpose can be anything – cultivating spirituality, a monetary goal, striving for happiness in a relationship, or anything else you truly yearn for. On the other hand, a **sincere purpose** is one that makes you feel accomplished and happy, and one that aligns your inner-most values with your desires.

To find your goal or sense of purpose, think of any area of your life you want to improve, and then find out what you truly want to achieve in that area. If you are thinking of your financial life, think of what you truly desire. Think about what you want your objective to be, and what its purpose serves. While doing that, consider your strengths and past accomplishments. This will allow you to set a personal, customized, and measureable goal.

Similarly, think of what sort of goals you want to set in terms of health, happiness, relationships, love, spirituality etc. Create many goals relating to different aspects of your life and then write them down. Regularly visit those goals so they can remain in your mind and sight. This way, you will stay focused on the bigger picture and whenever a setback in that area strikes you, it will bruise you but not throw you off balance.

Believe in Yourself Every Day

Start placing more faith in your yourself. You have already learnt how to discover your strengths and hone them, now all you must do is truly believe.

What is to believe you may ask? Well, what is to know the difference between your right hand and your left hand? What is it know that one dollar plus another dollar equals two dollars?

You may think that believing and knowing are two different things, but they truly are not.

If you believe in yourself as much as you are convinced that one plus one equals two, **you**

will be completely limitless. Your life will not only become whatever you want it to be, but you will change the world.

Believe that you have the power to change not only your life, but the lives of the many that surround you. Believe that a limitation is only a limitation if you perceive it as one. If you begin to believe that, you'll start to understand the undeniable truth that there are no such things as limitations. In consequence, once you begin to truly understand that, you will become **unstoppable**. The moment you start trusting your talents is the moment you know you have what it takes to move forward and emerge victorious even when all hell breaks loose.

From this day forward, frequently go through your achievements, and **appreciate** and **reward** yourself for your strengths. This way, you will stay confident even when adversity knocks you down.

Embrace Change

Being resilient does not just mean stubbornly holding on to what you believe in; it also means being flexible and adaptable to different circumstances. As is often the case, most adversities are not obstacles at all: **they are opportunities in disguise.** If you do not know how to embrace change, you are likely to miss an excellent opportunity only to realize your mistake later on.

Resilient people are flexible because they know the right way to react to a situation. To be truly resilient, **be flexible**. If you work on building the habits of <u>trying new things daily</u> and <u>seeing the good in every situation</u>, you will slowly nurture the habit of embracing change. This will improve your level of resilience and help you **seek opportunities**.

Work on these three keys and within a short time, your level of resilience will increase, you will become mentally stronger and happier, and you will experience the massive success that can only be experienced by a small group of people: **those who create the right change.**

Let's take this further by discussing honesty, as an ingredient for massive success in life.

Chapter 10
Be Honest: True Self

"The most daring thing is to be yourself and to do exactly what you want to do at that point in time and not to be worried with what other people are doing or what's popular." – Wiz Khalifa

The statement, "Honesty is the best policy", is 100% true. If you are not honest, you are lying and as Jon Stanley points out in his book, *The Millionaire Mind*, one lie usually has 15 supporting lies. If you lie once, you have to cover that lie by fabricating 15 other lies. Astonishing: so much hard work just to cover your tracks! Imagine what great results you could yield if you put that much effort into your work?

To stay happy, peaceful, and successful, it is important to be genuine, honest, and truthful in everything you do. When you do not have to lie about anything, you naturally feel peaceful at heart because you will be completely honest about everything.

Honesty brings you freedom in that you do not have to think a lot before saying anything. When you lie frequently, you are forcing yourself to recall the many stories associated with a lie to ensure you narrate it correctly each time; as you may guess, this will keep you from speaking freely.

In addition, honesty helps you transform your life for the better. When you are honest with **yourself** and **others**, you do not hide things; instead, you clarify what you want, and work on exactly what needs your attention. If you are a procrastinator, for instance, you will immediately address that issue. Instead of making excuses about your bad habit, you will continuously and consistently work to break it. This will eventually make you more efficient and, in turn, **successful**.

Similarly, honesty does wonders for you in every area of your life because when you are honest, you are not scared of hiding the truth.

This infuses serenity and happiness into your life.

Here is how you can build this habit.

Habit 21

The 3 Levels of Honesty

"Tell the truth boldly, whether it hurts or not. Never pander to weakness. If truth is too much for intelligent people and sweeps them away, let them go; the sooner the better." – Swami Vivekananda

In yogic terms, truth is called '**Satya**' and it is defined on three basic levels. To be honest, you need to work on these three levels:

Be honest about what you think

First, be honest about everything you think. If you are honest about your thoughts, you will be your true and genuine self, which will make others appreciate and respect you. Yes, sometimes your thoughts can upset them, but at least they will know your opinion is an honest one. To build the habit of being honest all the time, start being honest about what you think. Whenever you plan to act a certain way regarding a certain chore, think of what you truly want and be honest about your thoughts. Ultimately, this will help you take the right action.

Be honest about what you feel

Next, be honest about how you feel. This helps you better understand your emotions as well as what you want to do. For instance, if you are angry at your son because he wants to pursue marketing instead of finance but deep down you feel that you should let him do what he wants because that is what will bring him happiness, be honest about your feelings. Instead of focusing on what you want and being stubborn, be honest about your emotions and use them as a **cue** to take the right **action**.

Be honest about what you do

Lastly, be brutally honest about **what** you do and **want** to do. If you want your son to follow his heart, let him do so. If you want to do something you think will bring you happiness, be honest about it and do it right away. Moreover, always be honest about your line of work. Often, we are not pleased with our profession or do not feel it is a respectable one. We then fabricate lies about to it. Deep down, we cringe while doing this and do not feel at peace. This practice makes us shun our true self, which makes us put a false facade. To be happy inside out, be more honest about your profession. If you are a janitor, a dancer, or a waiter at a local restaurant, be honest about it because what you do is what helps you bring food into your house and that profession helps you sustain your lifestyle. If you are unhappy with what you do, find ways to improve it: **being dishonest about it will not help you**. Who knows, you could be one of the best chefs, dancers, or janitors, and might end up creating new connections with people who can help you grow in to your line of work.

Work your way through these three things and write your progress in your journal so you can track your performance. While you work on building the habit of honesty, avoid being blatant when conversing with people. It is fine to pinpoint their flaw if you feel doing so will help them improve, but if you feel that your comment will make them unhappy or lower their self-esteem, it is best to keep it to yourself.

For instance, if a friend dresses for a wedding in something you consider hideous, help her out and give her a few tips. Make sure she knows that you care, and that you're not just trying to bring her down. If you cannot do that, keep your advice to yourself so she does not feel miserable.

While honesty does instill happiness into your life, **spirituality** takes your happiness up a notch.

Chapter 11

Be Spiritually Connected

"When you are spiritually connected, you are not looking for occasions to be offended, and you are not judging and labeling others. You are in a state of grace in which you know you are connected to God and thus free from the effects of anyone or anything external to yourself." – Wayne Dyer

Spirituality is not something we can define in one single word, phrase, or sentence. It is a concept that varies from one person to another and one that brings a completely new meaning to one's life. Spirituality to you could be about bringing wisdom, curiosity, and creativity to your life; for your friend, it could be about connecting to their soul and tapping into their inner-power.

Spirituality is something that makes you feel alive and adds more substance and context to your life. You can choose to define it in any way you want. Regardless, the important thing is to nurture the habit of being spiritually connected; being so is a habit that emanates throughout all aspects of your life, and can improve and shine light onto anything and everything.

Spirituality increases your happiness levels and gives you the opportunity to truly appreciate your life. It improves and adds meaning and depth to your wisdom and sense of awareness and allows you to make the most of your life. Moreover, being spiritually connected allows you to effectively combat stress, which improves your psychological and physical well-being. Feeling 'spiritually lost' can and will greatly affect your propensity to be successful and happy. When you feel that there is something you are lacking or missing in life, you will find yourself not being happy for extended periods; your happiness will be episodic! Being a spiritually connected individual will never allow this to happen, for it gives one a sense of true understanding, knowledge, and hope, and will push the individual through any situation: **easy or difficult**.

Here is how you can develop this habit.

Habit 22
Spiritual Strategies

"Just as a candle cannot burn without fire, men cannot live without a spiritual life." –
Buddha

To foster a spiritual connection with yourself and the greater world, try the following strategies:

Meditate

Meditation is an excellent way to cultivate inner-peace and listen to your thoughts. The more you know about yourself, the better you can connect to your soul and enhance your spirituality. You have learnt how to meditate; put the knowledge to use and unlock your spirituality.

Be Vulnerable

Vulnerability is not a bad thing. In fact, being vulnerable is one of the things that can help unleash your spirituality. Being vulnerable means to know your position in each situation you face. If you do not know how to solve a crisis right in this moment, be vulnerable: accept that. If you feel the loss of a loved one has weakened you, acknowledge your feelings. Being vulnerable helps you know yourself better and the more insight you get into yourself, the better you work on self-improvement. Start being more vulnerable from this day onwards and soon, this practice will turn into a habit.

Connect with the Outside World

Connecting with the outside world is a great way to nurture the habit of spirituality. By observing and analyzing your environment and the different creatures and living-beings in it, such as humans, you can learn a lot about how this world truly operates. This understanding will increase your wisdom and, in turn, your sense of spirituality. Spend time with nature; quietly sit in a gathering and say nothing: just observe people and analyze all the things that occur around you. **Pay close attention, and analyze everything in detail.**

Find a Mentor

Finding a mentor is a great way to improve your spirituality. If you admire someone, and that person has achieved things you want to accomplish, learn from that person's experiences and life adventures; use the person's positive energy as your **guiding force**. It could be a celebrity, a historical figure, a fictional character, or even a family member. For instance, if you admire your mother for having put up with your father's anger management issues for 50 years, and you aspire to be emotionally strong as well, then maybe she could be your mentor regarding relationships. If you aspire to be a great entrepreneur like Richard Branson, you could learn from his life experiences and use the lessons to improve your financial and professional life. Pick as many mentors as you like and actively utilize their lessons, advices, and experiences as your guiding forces. This will allow you to improve as a person and enhance your spiritual connection to the world.

Start working on these guidelines and implement them regularly so you can unleash your spirituality and **completely** alter your life for the better.

In addition to building these powerful 'happy' habits, work on habits that invite financial prosperity into your life. While all the habits discussed previously will improve your financial life in different ways, there are certain habits that can specifically catapult you to **massive financial success**.

The next part of the book focuses solely on this goal.

Part 3

Habits of the Financially Prosperous

"Success means having the courage, the determination, and the will to become the person you believe you were meant to be."-George A. Sheehan

Financial success, like spirituality, is a relative concept: one that varies from person to person. Although we each define success differently, we shall discuss financial success because, in truth, money is required for **almost** everything in life.

Do you want to travel the world, and experience all the beautiful wonders it has to offer?

Do you want to surprise your wife of 20 years with something she has always wanted?

Do you feel compelled to provide your child with all the important things you may have been deprived of when you were young?

Unfortunately, the answers to these questions will almost always be one's regarding or revolving around money. This is just the world we live in today. But, it truly doesn't have to be difficult. All you need are the right tools, and I can guarantee you will be on the path to **great success**.

Financial success is not something many people know how to acquire. Nonetheless, being financially strong and successful is not a myth and is not something impossible; history and the present are full of financially successful and accomplished people who have carved their mark in the world and shown everyone the true capabilities of the **realized human being**. Albert Einstein, Thomas A. Edison, Warren Buffet, Tony Robbins, Richard Branson, Steve Jobs, Bill Gates, Oprah Winfrey, Mark Zuckerberg, and Michael Jordan are examples of prominent names who have accomplished amazing success and have created benchmarks for empowered lives.

Moreover, these accomplished people have also shown that success is about living life the way you want and empowering it so you never settle for what comes your way and instead carve **your own destiny**. They have clearly elaborated what Dharmesh Shah once said:

"Once upon a time, most people had to wait to be accepted, to get funded, to be promoted, to somehow be discovered. Not anymore! You can do almost everything you have the desire, skills, and drive to do: you do not need to wait for someone else to discover your talents. You get to discover yourself. The only thing holding you back is your willingness to take the leap, and try."

Success is all about believing in yourself, setting meaningful goals, and developing habits that help you reach your milestones and ultimately achieve those goals.

This part of the book focuses solely on habits that help you become a powerful, creative, and successful person; someone who finds it exciting and fulfilling to achieve all their dreams.

Before moving on, let me elaborate what a millionaire's mindset is:

What is a Millionaire's Mindset?

A millionaire's mindset is what separates the rich from the poor. It is the mindset possessed by the rich, successful, and famous and the one thing that brings enormous amount of prosperity into their life. This mindset is what helps them focus on their goal, and remain so for an extended period of time, no matter the amount or significance of obstacles that may come their way.

At the same time, this mindset is what helps them become more process oriented. Instead of losing heart when they fail to accomplish a certain goal, they gather up their hope and motivation, and focus on creating new strategies to help them achieve whatever they want. This way, they cherish each milestone, truly learn from them, and use them to increase their motivation to move forward.

The millionaire's mindset is what you need to cultivate to become an accomplished person. You can do this by following the guidelines given in this part of the book, and by working on the five powerful habits discussed as well.

Chapter 12
Invest

"Games are won by players who focus on the playing field –- not by those whose eyes are glued to the scoreboard." – Warren Buffett

Financial success and freedom does not come overnight and it is not something luck brings to you. It is something you invite by developing the right habits. Yes, like everything else, financial freedom and stability is dependent on habits.

Here are some amazing habits that can help you draw success and financial prosperity towards you.

To become financially strong and successful, the very first habit you must work on is to **invest your effort, energy, time, and money in the right sort of activities and people**. Often, we feel that we do not get the results we expect even though we put in so much effort, time, and money in the activity we expect to give us good returns. This is because we are investing in the wrong activities, people, and tasks; ones that will not bring us any substantial or significant result.

To get a good output and to be mentally and emotionally happy and peaceful, invest your effort and energies in the right sort of activities.

Habit 23

Invest in The Right Things

"Opportunities come infrequently. When it rains gold, put out the bucket, not the thimble" — Warren Buffett

Here are some things you should try to nurture this habit.

1 Start by creating a list of all professional and personal activities that you are involved in and analyze their effect on your life. Figure out the sort of return you are getting from each activity and if or not you truly want to be involved in it. For instance, if you are doing two jobs and one is not giving you the returns you expect but drains you of energy and makes you miserable, consider quitting and looking for another side income. (Earning multiple incomes is another habit we shall discuss in the book.) Similarly, analyze the effort you invest in everything you do especially activities that give you monetary return since we are discussing habits related to financial success. Create a new list of activities that give you good results, then commit to investing more time, effort, and money into those activities, and slowly cut back on those that do not give you a good output.

2 Next, **find out which activities are progressive and which ones are regressive**. Regressive activities pull you back and do not let you grow whereas the progressive ones take you forward towards growth and success. At this point, revisit the financial goals you created earlier and use them to figure out activities that can take you closer to your goal. For instance, if your financial goal is to open your chain of restaurants, taking cooking classes right now is an activity that could help you achieve that goal. If you have enrolled in a culinary program, that is a good progressive activity and one you should continue. However, if you are attending a singing program while you do not intend to become a singer and you know you have a terrible voice, that practice is a regressive one and is certainly a time waster for you. This practice and others like it are the practices you should eliminate from your routine so you can create more time and space for progressive habits and activities.

3 Spend time with successful people and those who positively influence you so you acquire good habits from them and use them to cultivate financial freedom. If you have a millionaire uncle, spend as much time with him as you can. The more you sit with him, the more you will learn things that will help you understand success and encourage you to put in effort to achieve your goals.

4 Reading books is a brilliant habit that helps you and never goes to waste. **Read consistently** and slowly reach the point where you can read at least two to three books a week. The more books you read, the wiser and more knowledgeable you will become, and the faster you shall move towards your goals. Read books on self-development and those that help you become the boss of your life because once you learn to take charge of your mind, you can truly do anything you want. You can climb a mountain, become a millionaire, beat all odds, and do absolutely anything you set your eyes on.

5 Take time to **analyze the activities you spend your money on** – are those activities giving you any return or is your investment going to waste? If you have invested in a savings plan, does it truly give you a good return, or is the interest too high? If you have invested money in a friend's business and are working as a sleeping partner, assess the return you get from that investment. Is that profit worth all your investment or is the return menial? Thinking in these lines helps you find out all the activities that give you poor return on investment (ROI), which helps you stop spending time and money on them and instead use your money on worthwhile activities instead.

6 In addition to doing the above, **practice creative visualization daily**. Creative visualization is a wonderful practice you should invest your time in because it will pave way for a better present and future.

Thinking big is essential to becoming successful. Creative visualization is an exercise that helps you think big and create many positive thoughts that draw positive and amazing experiences towards you. When you think big, you become hopeful of a better tomorrow and feel confident and capable of objectifying your goals. This gives you the courage to follow your heart and pursue your dreams. To practice creative visualization, sit somewhere peaceful and think of one of your goals. Close your eyes and imagine yourself achieving that goal. If your goal is to open a school that helps autistic children groom themselves, imagine having opened that school and running it successfully. Add many tiny details like colors, gestures, expressions, background sounds, and noises in the scenario: make it feel alive. Keep thinking about it for a good 15 to 20 minutes and do so every day at any time you feel comfortable. Practice visualization at that time every day so you can cultivate punctuality and consistency. With time, you will develop the habit of practicing creative visualization and thinking big.

7 One more practice you need to turn into a habit is **creative thinking** so you unleash your creative skills and build many ideas. Your ideas birth new creations or bring innovations to already existing inventions. The more ideas you think of and the more you polish them, the better your chances are of landing on a fantastic idea that could lead you to a breakthrough. When Thomas Edison began creating inventions, it took him about 1000 failures to reach a point where he received any appreciation and recognition. Had he stopped thinking when the world rejected his first idea, we would have never gotten the electric light bulb and many others of Edison's amazing creations that add convenience to our lives today. Thomas Edison never stopped thinking; he became a machine of creative ideas. This ability is what helped him think big and great, which is how he unleashed his inner potential. You need to do the same.

To build this habit, here are a few things that you can try:

Never Discount Even Your Craziest Ideas

Make it a point to jot down any unusual or even mundane idea you get in your journal and then analyze and explore it later on. At times, your craziest or silliest idea can lead to brilliance. Instagram, the wonderful app we all love and use, was initially a 'check-in' app. However, users did not receive it very well. Instead of discarding that idea because it did not gather the response its creators, Kevin Systrom and Mike Krieger, expected, they honed it and turned into the amazing application we cannot stop using. If they had dismissed that idea, we would never have created this revolutionary application.

Hence, never ever throw away your ideas. Instead, record them, experiment with them, and explore them later so you can use them to create something inspirational. Whenever you spend some quality alone time, let your mind free, keep your goal in sight, and think of whatever comes to your mind. You can think of any other ideas too that may be irrelevant to your goal because it is good to create many ideas, and experiment with a number of things so you can build many meaningful goals and achieve many amazing things.

Learn as Much as You Humanly Possibly Can

The most innovative and successful people are amazing learners and have a knack for using the lessons they learned to create something. Take Steve Jobs example. While talking about him, Walter Isaacson once said, *"He (Jobs) connected the humanities to the sciences, creativity to technology, and arts to engineering. There were greater technologists and certainly better designers and artists, but no one else in our era could better fire wire together poetry and processors in a way that jolted innovation."*

This quote alone is enough to describe Steve Jobs' amazing talents for combining the different lessons and skills he had acquired throughout the course of his life to come up with the fantastic idea of Macintosh and then give it the shape of reality.

To follow Job's footsteps and the footsteps of many other brilliant people like him, start **learning**. For that, **read** as much as you can on many topics. Read on sports, movies, history, geography, botany, science, technology, human mind, psychology, biology, physics, and absolutely anything you come across.

Start following these guidelines so you put your effort, energies, time, and money only in the right sort of things. This will slowly inculcate in you the habit of spending only on the right activities, businesses, and people. This shall help you live an empowered life.

To welcome financial freedom, the next habit you need to work on is to plan for your success. Let us discuss that next.

Chapter 13
Plan for Success

"Being busy does not always mean real work. The object of all work is production or accomplishment and to either of these ends there must be forethought, system, planning, intelligence, and honest purpose, as well as perspiration. Seeming to do is not doing." – Thomas A. Edison

Planning for success is an important part of accomplishing your dreams. The quote above is 100% true: Planning is the one practice that helps you immediately understand what you should do to make your future better and as desired. For instance, if you plan to become a billionaire in the future, you must plan for that success right now. Unless you know exactly what you must do to achieve that goal, you cannot accomplish it.

Planning here refers to first crafting a plan of action, allocating time to working on it, and then planning your routine activities so that everything you do takes you closer to the many goals you have set for yourself, in particular your financial goals. If you do not plan how to achieve your goals, you will never get a sense of direction and without a clear direction, you will move haphazardly.

To clarify what to do and steadily move towards fulfilling your lifelong goals, planning is imperative.

Before we discuss that, here is an exercise you should do:

Clarify Your Long-term Financial Goal

First take your journal and consider your financial goal. Analyze your goal in detail; the goal here is to figure out if you truly want to pursue it. To find that out, check for four things.

- ✓ First, find out if that goal is relevant to something you are passionate about or good at and something you can talk about for hours without getting annoyed or bored. This is important because when you are enthusiastic about something or are exceptionally good at something, you will enjoy pursuing that goal and will never lose focus in it.

✓ Secondly, that goal should center on the environment you grew up in as a child. This is important because the environment you grow up in shapes your personality and if you integrate that element into your goal or destiny, you will be more committed to its pursuit. For instance, if you grew up in a violent neighborhood/environment and saw your father behave cruelly towards your mother and you are passionate about human rights, you could become a human rights activist and help victims of domestic violence get justice.

✓ Thirdly, think of the stranger feedback you get about your strengths and things you are good at. No stranger will lie to you about your qualities; strangers give you an honest overview so think of what your acquaintances, colleagues, or people you are less involved with you think of you and compliment you at. For instance, I know of someone complimented on being a good reader who grew up around educationists and had a passion for speaking on self-development. Using these cues and the fourth one that I will just discuss below, he determined that his destiny was to use his knowledge to empower people and became a notable self-help expert.

✓ The fourth factor you need to figure out is actually very simple: consider what you have been doing on the professional front for the past few years consecutively. If you have been working as a marketer for the past three years or as a teacher for the last decade, naturally, you have built a certain skill set. It would be futile not to use that skill set. Therefore, consider that skill set when planning your long-term goal. Keep that factor in mind along with the other three and use them to find your destiny or ultimate financial goal that gives your life meaning.

After identifying your destiny, it is time to plan how to achieve it. The stages for planning we shall discuss below are the steps you should follow each time you embark on a new journey to achieve something, whenever you set a new goal and even otherwise in your routine to do different tasks on time and to accomplish different happiness and relationship related goals.

Here is how you can inculcate this habit into your life.

Habit 24
The Habit of Planning

"Planning is bringing the future into the present so that you can do something about it now." – Alan Lakein

1 Once you have settled on your ultimate goal, take a good look at it, and then chop it down into lots of bite-sized pieces. The magnitude of a big goal makes it seem overwhelming. For instance, you may want to become a millionaire, but the moment you think about it, you lose your calm because that gigantic goal is intimidating or overwhelming. However, once you break it down into steps such as first start a small home-based bakery, slowly expand the business and get a shop on rent, and then slowly purchase that store and expand to another city, it becomes easier to digest. It no longer seems impossible to you; rather, you gain clarity on what you need to do to accomplish that goal. As they say, success is a product of many small accomplishments. Think of what your goal is and then slash it into many tiny pieces so you have something to do every day to achieve that big goal. As you break your goal into numerous smaller, doable tasks, write them down in your journal so you have a list of all the things you need to do to meet a certain goal.

2 Have a short-term and a medium-term goal that takes you towards your long-term goal. If your long-term goal is to become an internationally renowned self-help public speaker, your medium-term goal could be to become a nationally acclaimed public speaker and short-term goal could be to gain recognition on state level. After identifying your milestones, take your short-term goal and determine how to accomplish it. Define that goal in detail so you know exactly what it entails and peg it to a timeline so you know when it is due.

3 Next, plan how to make time for working on the tasks relating to a goal so you can get started with your plan of action. Remind yourself of the bigger picture you must fulfill and use it as motivation to improve your time management skills. Create daily, weekly, and monthly **To-do lists** related to the tasks you have to do to accomplish your short-term goal. Prioritize tasks that result in maximum output. Also, assign one difficult task to every day or every two to three days depending on its nature. Do that task at the beginning of your day because when you '**eat an ugly frog in the morning**,' you know nothing worse can happen, and when you accomplish something challenging, you become inspired to work on several other tasks too.

4 Every day before doing to bed, revisit your To-do list for the next day so you plan beforehand and prepare for the next day before it starts. This also helps you make necessary changes to your routine and To-do lists as you experience different situations; this makes you adaptable and resilient. When you do this daily, you nurture the habit and use it to plan a better future.

5 After going through the planning stage, the next thing is to work on the plan of action. To do that, try the following strategies and turn them into habits so you never find it difficult to work on your goals:

Set Compelling Rewards

Upon achieving your set goals, give yourself rewards you enjoy. For instance, each time you work on a difficult task, treat yourself to a nice massage at your favorite spa or buy yourself a good book. Write down these rewards next to a goal and make sure to check both when you start working on that task. This encourages you to move forward towards that task and complete it right on time.

Write Yourself Positive Short Notes

Write yourself notes that motivate you to become progressive and complete tasks on time. Pin these tasks at different places of your house and workplace. Think your fridge, dining table, work desk, your office main wall, white board in your cubicle etc. Each time you glance at those notes, you will experience a surge of encouragement that which will push you forward so you stop thinking and start working instead.

Try the 2-Minute Hack

Whenever you have a seemingly difficult task to work on, try the 2-minute hack. Tell yourself you will only work on a task for 2 minutes and keep tricking yourself to work for another round of 2 minutes until you complete about 30% of the task. With this hack, you will not even realize how easier it becomes to work on even the most challenging tasks. Try it a couple of times and you will be hooked on it for good, which will consequently turn into your habit.

Divide a Chore into Different Parts

Divide chores into different parts and work on each part for about 30 to 40 minutes or even more depending on its nature. Once the given time lapses, stop working on that part, and take a short 5 to 10 minute break. When you know you are pressed for time, you focus on the task better and do not become distracted. This helps you complete tasks fast in less time, which helps you manage time like a pro.

Manage Distractions

Moreover, start managing distractions more efficiently. Create a list of all the different things, activities, people, and anything else that has a tendency to distract you when you are doing an important chore or working on your plan of action. Your distractions could be anything from being tempted to binge watch movies on Netflix, to talking to a friend for hours (live or on social media/IM), to napping the moment you must work on a chore.

After listing all your probable distractions, the ones you succumb to regularly, find ways to combat them. What could you do to tackle a certain distraction? What can you do to stop binge watching movies so you can focus on work instead? Ask yourself these questions and you will soon come up with appropriate and effective fixes to all your distractions.

For instance, you could firmly start saying no to all the people who incessantly bother you with their demands whenever you sit to do your own work. If you have a habit of pleasing others, you probably prioritize others and their demands more than your work. If this is the case, it is time you started saying no to all those people so you prioritize yourself. As for the friends who have your best interests at heart but have a habit of showing up every now and then just because they want to be with you, let them know you will hang out with them once you are done with your work. After dealing with them, focus on only your work and nothing else.

Similarly, to manage distractions such as incessantly playing games on your phone, using Social Media, or watching movies, switch off your phone or put it in Airplane mode when you are working, block Facebook and other social media sites and apps for a while, and take the television out of your room so you can only concentrate on work.

You could also put a 'do not disturb' label at the door to your working area', install apps or web browser extensions to limit your access to certain sites (e.g. Leech Block for Firefox and StayFocusd for Chrome are great for this), put on headphones even when not listening to anything etc.

At first, blocking distractions will be hard and you will face a lot of inner resistance that will keep you from doing so. Because you are committed to self-improvement and becoming a winner in every aspect of your life, commit to blocking the distractions: the first time is the hardest and if you can do it once, you can do it repeatedly.

The next time you face the same distractions, remember how you battled them with courage and you will instantly become motivated to do the same.

Employ these time management hacks daily and in no time, you will find yourself beating procrastination and working on your plan of action like a pro.

Now that you know how to develop the habit of planning your work, and how to build the habit to beat procrastination so you implement your plan of action, let us discuss another important habit that is a surefire way to bring in amazing success into your life: the habit of being 100% confident and always focused on your goals.

Chapter 14

Develop Focus and Confidence

"Trust yourself. Create the kind of self that you will be happy to live with all your life. Make the most of yourself by fanning the tiny, inner sparks of possibility into flames of achievement." – Golda Meir

Ask various rich men and women how they became successful and you will surely find one commonality: **killer focus and amazing self-confidence.** You cannot fulfill your dreams and become a magnet for wealth, abundance, and success until you work on these two elements.

Killer focus helps you concentrate on your goals. When nothing can divert your attention, you focus only on what is important to you. This way, even when things do not go your way, you find a way out of the problem because you have not thought about anything else but your goal. Hence, a killer focus is an essential tool to have in your wealth arsenal.

To develop killer focus, you need self-confidence. If you closely analyze famous politicians, celebrities, public speakers, rulers and leaders of the world, you will discover that all of them were and are brilliantly confident. They had/have unbelievable self-belief. This confidence is what gave/gives them the ability and strength to fully believe in themselves, constantly take action towards their dreams, and gracefully move past adversities.

Let us now discuss how to build the habit of becoming confident 24/7 and staying focused on what is most important to you.

Habit 25

Nurture the Habit of Staying Focused and Confident

"Have faith in your skills. Doubt kills more dreams than failure ever will."
— Suzy Kassem

Focus on Your Dreams

One major reason why many of us do not get what we aspire for is that we focus on the wrong things. Instead of focusing on our goals, we focus more on all the troubles we will encounter on our way and all the obstacles that may come our way. As mentioned before, the sort of thoughts you harbor and sport bring exactly those sort of experiences your way. If you focus on difficulties, you will bring more challenges your way.

To acquire success, you must focus on the things you want in your life and nothing else. If you want to be a millionaire through opening your multinational chain of restaurants, you must remain focused on just that and not the difficulties you may experience.

Get into the habit of writing down your goal and all the things you want with respect to it every day on a fresh page in your journal. Write them down several times and read them aloud each time you write those things.

For instance, if you want a big mansion, three luxury cars, a million dollars in your bank account, and a huge ranch, write down these objectives on a page several times. Doing this practice for a good 15 minutes will help you focus more than before. By the time you finish this practice, you will feel more enthusiastic about your goal. Avoid thinking of things you do not want and things that may scare you away from pursuing your goal.

Get Up Early

Getting up early will give you that much needed 25th hour of the day: a very important time to do much of what you haven't been able to do within your 'normal' waking hours.

Being an early bird is a powerful trait that aids significantly in the improvement and sustenance of your focus. Early morning, there are hardly any distractions to bother you. Not only this, but by waking up a few hours earlier than usual, you are giving yourself the time and opportunity to be productive, create ideas, and exercise other successful habits: actions and behaviors that will slowly but surely push you towards living the life of your dreams. Along with this, when you wake up fresh after a good night's sleep, you are much more mentally clear and energized. If you pay attention to your thought patterns, you will notice that mental tensions increase and intensify as the day progresses. Since you are more relaxed, mentally energized, and much less distracted during early morning, that is the right time to being working on your goals and constructing your plan for success.

If you examine the lives of accomplished people like Barrack Obama, Ursula Burns, the CEO of Xerox, Tim Armstrong, CEO of AOL and Indra Nooyi, CEO of PepsiCo, you will notice that all of them rise early. This habit is one practiced by all prosperous people all over the world. In fact, many of these people are often quick to point out that waking up early has greatly contributed to their success. To skyrocket your focus and prosperity, become an early bird too. To do that, start sleeping early. Instead of wasting the night and going to bed after midnight, develop the habit of sleeping between 8pm to 11pm.

If you suffer from insomnia or find it difficult to initiate sleep easily and quickly, habitually exercise four hours before your sleep time. Exercise releases feel-good hormones such as dopamine and serotonin into your body. These hormones invigorate and calm you, which reduces stress and allows you to rest much easier. Moreover, exercise also works out your muscles, which exhausts and tires you before your bedtime. When you are tired, you sleep easier.

In addition, develop a soothing pre-sleep routine that helps you unwind before your sleeping time. An hour or two before your planned sleep time, do something soothing such as taking a warm shower, reading a soothing or motivation book, or watching something that calms you down. This will relax your stressed nerves, which will help you sleep quicker.

Become Involved in the Process

Another habit you must work on is becoming process oriented. When you are process oriented, you remain focused on your goal without succumbing to overwhelm. Instead of focusing solely on the rewards, you become much more infatuated and in love with the entire systematic process itself. When this is the case, you love what you do. And when you love what you do, you perfect it. You become the master of it, and you take it to a level it has **never** been before: no matter what it may be.

Not only this, but you also begin to truly enjoy the little accomplishments and milestones that you achieve, and your mind never strays away from the much more important "bigger picture" of your pursuit.

To become process oriented, write in your journal your daily activities as well as how well you perform certain tasks. Go through your journal entry before sleeping and go through the entire journal once weekly. This helps you track your achievements, which slowly increases your self-belief and focus.

Gain Followers

Social media is all the rage nowadays and it would be silly not to take advantage of this tool. While you may find this hilarious right now, social media can actually help you skyrocket your focus and confidence.

How, you ask? If you publicize your work on your social media accounts, interact with your existing followers, and share your work to gain more followers, you will soon have a plethora of followers who will back you up. Their backing and support will make you feel great about yourself, which will enhance your confidence. Moreover, they will also help you stay focused on your goals.

When you **make your plans public**, people will ask about them and when they question you about your future endeavors, you feel a little pressure to give them good news of success. This keeps you focused on your work and helps you eventually actualize your goals.

Moreover, habitually **seek feedback** from your followers about how well you are working towards the accomplishment of your goals and how good your work is. If you have launched a product, offer a few followers free samples in exchange for feedback. Feedback helps you improve your work, which breathes more confidence into you. When you see people appreciating your work, it enhances your self-belief. Moreover, it also improves your focus because when you know you are capable of doing good work, you improve your effort and desire to do amazing work.

Help Others Succeed

A good reason why successful people are increasingly confident is that they help spread kindness, love, and success around. How does this help you skyrocket your confidence? Well, when you help people accomplish their goals, you naturally feel proud of yourself. This in turn increases both your level of focus and confidence.

Therefore, develop the habit of helping others fulfill their goals and tasks. Find out who in your family and social circle is struggling with achieving his or her goals and then reach out to that person. Ask that person about his or her goal and the help he or she needs to fulfill those goals. Analyze the situation and figure out how you can help. Once you come up with probable solutions, communicate your ideas with that person, and then start helping that person become better.

For instance, if your sibling has a brilliant idea of launching an innovative startup, but is struggling with accumulating enough funds to do so, perhaps you could lend him some money as a silent business partner. If your friend needs help understanding the nitty-gritty of a business you are involved in, you could help him with the research and understanding part. You can help people in any way you want; just remember not to be cocky about it and to stay modest.

If you implement these habits into your life, you will develop killer focus and confidence. Not only this, but you will be on a sure-fire path towards acquiring the millionaire's mindset: a mental tool that allows you to prosper and grow **like nothing else.**

To increase your chances of success, you also need to work on developing another crucial habit: prioritizing delayed gratification.

Chapter 15

Seek Delayed Gratification

"Success awaits those who steadfastly commit to any requisite sacrifice" — Ken Poirot

Developing the habit of seeking delayed gratification is essential for you to succeed in life. If you do not build this habit, you will always seek instant gratification and lose motivation to work for long-term goals as soon as you enjoy some accomplishment in the present.

Moreover, when you prioritize instant gratification, you lose hope very quickly whenever you face a setback or two. This makes you procrastinate and quit the pursuit of your ultimate goals. **The truth is**: success does not come that easy; it (success) is a lifelong process that takes time to fulfill. To achieve the goal you have been aspiring for a long time, you must be fully involved in every step. You need to think long-term and pursue delayed gratification. Only when you build this habit can you learn to let go of instant gratification and become inspired to work for your very best.

To help you understand the importance of this habit, consider the story of Mr. Soichiro Honda, the renowned owner and founder of the popular Honda Motors: a man who accomplished amazing success because of his genuine love for delayed gratification, and his invigorated ability to remain focused on the "long-term."

Soichiro Honda's Success Story

In 1938 while Mr. Honda was studying in school, he decided to invest all his earnings in a workshop. Over there, he started to work on the idea of a piston ring he planned to sell one day to the Toyota Corporation. He burned the midnight oil, worked arduously, and finally produced the piston rings he desired. When he presented those to Toyota, they told him the rings did not meet the company's quality criteria.

Had Mr. Honda opted for instant gratification, he would have instantly backed down and would have pursued something else. However, he had different plans for himself and he decided to stick to the decision he took in the first place. He kept working on those piston rings and presented them to Toyota again after two years. This time, he received his dream contract. However, right when he thought things had started becoming bright for him, the Japanese government suffered from a war threat and began gearing up for it. The government did not oblige his request for the cement supplies he required to build his factory to manufacture the piston rings. Mr. Honda could have quit then too but he did not: he persevered.

He then planned to build his factory using his own concrete that he created with his team. However, he faced another setback when major parts of his manufacturing facility became casualties of war (bombed). Instead of dampening his spirits, that setback presented him with another opportunity: he rallied all his team members and picked up gasoline cans thrown by the US fighters. He used those cans to gather all the raw materials he needed to manufacture the piston rings.

Mr. Honda survived this setback too, but fate had something else in store for him. An earthquake hit the city and leveled his entire factory. At that point, Mr. Honda sold the piston manufacturing facility to Toyota. Once the war was over, a huge gasoline shortage hit Japan and Soichiro Honda could not even get food to feed his family.

In desperate times, he created a bicycle to which he attached a tiny motor. He created several other motorized bikes that he started to sell and ultimately built a plant to manufacture them. He did not have enough capital to produce those bikes so he decided to get help from other bike manufacturers in the country.

Since his bike was a heavy one, nobody was ready to invest in that sample. He worked on his idea again and created a lightweight version of his idea and when he presented that prototype to bike manufacturers, his idea instantly became a massive hit. That one idea brought Mr. Honda amazing success and he eventually built the Honda Corporation that now employs more than 100,000 people in Japan and the US.

While this story is quite a long one, if you read it keenly, you will understand why Mr. Soichiro Honda succeeded in the end: because he knew he had to stay committed to his decision and had to think long-term. He knew delayed gratification is what would help him in the end. He encountered many instances that could have provided him instant gratification or provided him with an escape from all the excruciating troubles he faced in the present. Did he back out? No, he did not. He knew he had to persevere and sustain his grit until he attained success; this is what he did – his results speak for themselves.

If like Mr. Honda, you too want unimaginable success, here is how you can nurture the habit of seeking delayed gratification.

Habit 26

Build the Habit of Thinking Long-Term

"Adopt the pace of nature: her secret is patience." – Ralph Waldo Emerson

1 Firstly, build the habit of never losing sight of your goal. If you work on the habits that inculcate killer focus, you will find it easy to think long-term and always **focus on future**.

2 Secondly, never spend too much time celebrating your milestones. If you achieve a short-term goal or complete a task that leads to your goal, that is wonderful. However, **if you continue celebrating that victory, you may become too satisfied with your present accomplishments and least bothered with pursuing your long-term goal**. To ensure this does not happen, rapidly move forward after ˋcelebrating your milestones for a couple of hours. If you just achieved your short-term goal, throw a small party and invite your friends. As soon as the party is over, get back to work. Building this habit will take time, but as soon as you nurture this, you will never settle for instant gratification: **you will always pursue delayed gratification**.

3 Thirdly, make your long-term goal your **highest responsibility**. This means you should feel obligated to your goals. Obviously, the process that takes you to the long-term goal is what you should be involved in, but you should never forget your highest responsibility and obligation. Thinking long-term and of the future does not mean you should stop becoming process oriented. It just means that although you should be involved in every aspect of the process, you should also never lose sight of your ultimate obligation: **to fulfill your true goal**. To build the habit of staying committed to your highest responsibility, speak to yourself about your goal as much as you can. If you performed a task well, say something like "Well done, I'm going to keep working like that so I eventually reach my final goal." If you made a mistake and faltered, instead of being harsh, say something comforting such as "Faltering is fine. Everyone makes mistakes. I'm going to get back up right now and strive to meet my goal." When you speak to yourself in this manner, you never forget your ultimate responsibility and always think of your future.

These simple practices, if followed, can make your life amazing and can help you carve your name in history. To attain your goals, it is important to save money and pay yourself. The last chapter will discuss this final habit.

Chapter 16
Pay Yourself First

"A part of all I earn is mine to Keep." –
George S. Clason

Achieving a goal does not happen magically. Unfortunately, to fulfill your financial goals and manifest your creative ideas, you **must** have monetary funds. In truth, unless you have the money to support your ideas, you will find it very difficult to move forward. If Mr. Honda did not have his savings, he would have not been able to invest in that workshop that paved way for his success. If Warren Buffet did not have enough money to invest in that company when he was just 12, he would not be where he is today. Therefore, in most cases, fulfilling goals and achieving financial prosperity requires having pre-existing monetary reserves. For you to create a monetary reserve, you must begin **paying yourself first**.

Paying yourself first means you should start saving for your goals, and preparing yourself for financial freedom. Many of us cannot work on our dream goals right away because we must fulfill other obligations to our family and household. However, if we save for our goals, we can slowly accumulate a descent reserve that will give us the opportunity to manifest our dreams and visions into our reality. In other words, we can use those savings to work on our **million dollar ideas**.

Additionally, savings also come in handy when, God forbid, troubling times come knocking. If our income flow stops or something disturbs it, we can resort to those savings as we look for another source of income. For instance, you may be working on your ultimate and passion-filled goal right now, but if you do not save money, you may lose everything you have built if you encounter any financial issues. However, if you do start to save, you will have reserves you can use to support yourself at that time and you will have greater ease of mind while striving to achieve your goals.

Whatever the scenario is, the truth is that paying yourself first is a great habit that can help you accomplish and reach your financial goals.

Here is how you can build this habit.

Habit 27

Nurture the Habit of Paying Yourself First

"Investing in yourself is the best investment you will ever make. it will not only improve your life, it will improve the lives of all those around you." — Robin S. Sharma

Save For Your Goals

Start with saving a little for your goals. To do that, create a list of your basic and fixed expenses – all the expenses you cannot control. These should include food, utility bills, basic clothing, house rent (if you live in a rental), tax, gas (if you drive a car), and other similar expenses. Calculate your earnings and find what portion of your income goes to these expenses. Of whatever remains, save at least 10% of it; you can use the rest for all your other leisure related expenses.

As your income increases, increase the percentage of your savings to 12% then 15% and so on until you save about 50% of whatever you are left with after spending on all your fixed expenses. This habit can be a tough one to build especially if you are a shopaholic or if you never developed a saving culture. However, if you take baby steps, you can nurture this helpful, healthy habit.

If saving 10% of your leftover earnings is tough, start with saving around $50 a month or even $25. Once you can easily save $50 each month and maintain this habit for three to four months, slowly move to saving $60 or $75 a month. When you sustain that habit for a few months, move to saving $100 a month. Analyze your savings each month and when you see that tiny amount growing each day, you will feel amazing.

Make sure you do not spend that saving on anything unimportant. You can dedicate a portion of it to things like medical emergencies but other than that, you should not touch your savings.

Create Multiple Incomes

The second habit you need to work on is to establish **multiple income** streams. Adequately meeting all household responsibilities, saving money, and keeping your family happy with just one means of income is often not easy. Not many of us have great 9 to 5 jobs that pay us handsomely. Most of us have to make do with menial paying jobs that drain our energy to engage in another job. What should we do in this case? How can you establish multiple income streams in that scenario? Well, that is not too difficult.

If you are holding a 9-5 job, you can still earn through multiple means if you start invest a bit of your savings in some businesses. You can buy stocks online or you can start a small online business. Many online businesses such as blogging or drop shipping are easy enough to set up and run without exerting too much effort or time. You could even self-publish a book on Amazon Kindle, make an app, which makes you passive income, invest in equipment rental business etc. Find out more about side businesses and opt for one or two that provide you with another revenue stream.

If you have a knack for writing and do not find that task too difficult, blogging is a good option. All you have to do is set your own blog by selecting a niche you would like to venture into, produce valuable and meaningful content, and then spread the word around to publicize your blog.

Once you have enough traffic, you can sell your own eBooks or can work as an affiliate marketer to make money. However, if you enjoy selling things and love the idea of having your own eStore, you could venture into drop shipping, another great model that allows you to sell goods to others without going through the hassle of stocking the goods yourself. Pick any of these options and search for more so you can increase your income. You can learn more about making passive income here and here.

Watch Your Health

Your health is your greatest asset. Without it, you cannot work as you would want to, will probably spend a lot of money at the hospital, are likely to be discouraged, might lose hope and put your loved ones through a lot of emotional, financial and psychological stress. To ease and perhaps evade the burden, it is important that you take care of your health the same way you would protect a newborn. Go for regular health checkups, follow any medication you are given, eat well, engage in physical exercises and avoid doing things that put your health at risk. Moreover, you can protect your wealth and loved ones from the financial burden of meeting hospital expenses (if they occur) by having a good health insurance cover. This will take care of much of your treatment bills something which will ensure you don't end up in a worse financial state after you get out from the hospital.

There is a reason why the wealthy people spend a huge part of their income on insurance, healthcare and other avenues that ensure that they protect their wealth and build it even the more with greater ease.

The Atlantis puts it best:

"It's boring to point out that having more money affords you more food, more clothes, more housing, and more cars. But the richest families actually spend less on food, clothes, housing, and cars than the poorest families as a share of their income. The real difference between the rich and the poor is that the rich spend a larger share of their much larger income on insurance, education, and when you drill into the housing component, mortgages – all of which are directly related to building wealth, preserving wealth, and passing it down in the form of inheritance of direct investments in the lives of their children."

Work on implementing these guidelines and in no time, you will have set a good monetary reserve for yourself and will be in a position to use this to achieve your financial goals.

Conclusion

We have come to the end of the book. Congratulations and thank you for read it to the end. I believe you now understand how to prime yourself for the success that you are looking for.

The truth is; success of any type does not come easy; however, if you develop and nurture the 27 habits we have discussed in this book, **you will achieve mind-boggling success.**

To develop and nurture these habits, go slow and work on any one habit at a time following the guidelines given in the introductory part of this guide. Do not overwhelm yourself by working on numerous habits at once: this will only deplete your willpower.

Remember, slow and steady wins the race.

Also, thank you very much for reading this. I hope this book was able to instill in you the sense of understanding and knowledge I spoke about in the beginning. If you feel it truly helped you, show your **gratitude** by leaving a review. I would greatly **appreciate** it☺

Click here to leave a review!

Printed in Poland
by Amazon Fulfillment
Poland Sp. z o.o., Wrocław